NEW DIRECTIONS FOR HIGHE

MW00909841

Martin Kramer, *University of California, Berkeley*
EDITOR-IN-CHIEF

Strengthening the College Major

Carol Geary Schneider
Association of American Colleges

William Scott Green
University of Rochester

EDITORS

Number 84, Winter 1993

JOSSEY-BASS PUBLISHERS
San Francisco

STRENGTHENING THE COLLEGE MAJOR
Carol Geary Schneider, William Scott Green (eds.)
New Directions for Higher Education, no. 84
Volume XXI, Number 4
Martin Kramer, Editor-in-Chief

© 1993 by Jossey-Bass Inc., Publishers. All rights reserved.

No part of this issue may be reproduced in any form—except for a brief quotation (not to exceed 500 words) in a review or professional work—without permission in writing from the publishers.

Microfilm copies of issues and articles are available in 16mm and 35mm, as well as microfiche in 105mm, through University Microfilms Inc., 300 North Zeeb Road, Ann Arbor, Michigan 48106-1346.

LC 85-644752   ISSN 0271-0560   ISBN 1-55542-723-5

NEW DIRECTIONS FOR HIGHER EDUCATION is part of The Jossey-Bass Higher and Adult Education Series and is published quarterly by Jossey-Bass Inc., Publishers, 350 Sansome Street, San Francisco, California 94104-1342 (publication number USPS 990-880). Second-class postage paid at San Francisco, California, and at additional mailing offices. POST-MASTER: Send address changes to New Directions for Higher Education, Jossey-Bass Inc., Publishers, 350 Sansome Street, San Francisco, California 94104-1342.

SUBSCRIPTIONS for 1993 cost $47.00 for individuals and $62.00 for institutions, agencies, and libraries.

EDITORIAL CORRESPONDENCE should be sent to the Editor-in-Chief, Martin Kramer, 2807 Shasta Road, Berkeley, California 94708-2011.

Cover photograph and random dot by Richard Blair/Color & Light © 1990.

Manufactured in the United States of America. Nearly all Jossey-Bass books, jackets, and periodicals are printed on recycled paper that contains at least 50 percent recycled waste, including 10 percent postconsumer waste. Many of our materials are also printed with vegetable-based ink; during the printing process, these inks emit fewer volatile organic compounds (VOCs) than petroleum-based inks. VOCs contribute to the formation of smog.

CONTENTS

EDITORS' NOTES

In the United States, contemporary campus debates about educational goals and curricula are governed by a curious imbalance between the ambitious scope of the discussion and the distinct constraints imposed upon the solution. Typically, faculty committees and academic administrators begin a process of academic renewal by asking fundamental questions about the nature of liberal education:

What should an educated person know to function as a contributing member of our democratic, diverse, technologically advanced society?

What must the college graduate know to participate in the global community in the fast-approaching twenty-first century?

What intellectual capacities are required for full participation in both our national life and the global community?

What values are required for this participation?

What kinds of learning will help students develop the needed knowledge, intellectual capacities, and values?

How can we impart to graduates the ability to continue their learning across the life span?

Questions of this sort, once posed, invariably engage an institution's faculty in a searching exploration of their educational mission, the world around them, their own values, scholars' different ways of knowing, and students' diverse modes of learning. Each institution's answer to these questions, achieved with unavoidable struggles as competing worldviews collide, is then offered as a framework that both expresses the core values of the institution and provides a guide for all students' learning.

In the long history of Western conversations about higher learning, Bruce Kimball (1986) has identified two basic models for liberal education. The first, prevalent in nineteenth-century U.S. colleges, sees higher education as the acquisition of knowledge and values needed to provide leadership in the graduate's own community. The second model, more characteristic of research eras, views liberal learning as an orientation to fundamental ways of knowing, or modes of inquiry, by which people make sense of the physical world, society, culture, and the nature of human existence.

Contemporary curricular frameworks usually combine elements of both models. Across the country, at colleges and universities alike, recently crafted guidelines for the baccalaureate degree call for students to acquire specific kinds of societal and cultural knowledge and such intellectual capacities as critical thinking and problem solving, and historical, scientific, moral, and aesthetic reasoning, as well as competence in both written and spoken

1

communication. Many such campus models for student learning are visionary; virtually all are ambitious in their conception of the arts that constitute an education for the modern world.

General Education Myopia

The anomaly emerges, however, when we contrast the reach of institutions' expressed educational goals with the amount of curricular time these same colleges and universities actually assign to achieving these goals. Even though campus debates about the purposes of education overtly address both the whole person and the whole structure of baccalaureate learning, almost without exception these educational reviews are conducted to specify goals for general education. And while definitions of general education vary from institution to institution, there is near unanimity across U.S. higher education about general education's modest estate within the larger curricular territory. On all but a handful of campuses, general education courses make up about one-third of the total four-year curriculum. They almost never exceed half of it.

These debates about overarching goals for learning are therefore, in effect, reviews of goals for about 35 to 40 percent of the curriculum. Operating on a time-honored distinction between educational breadth (the purpose of general education) and educational depth (the purpose of a concentration, or major), faculty members reviewing general goals for higher learning work within a constraining framework that says, in effect, that overarching educational goals will be addressed in the fraction of a student's curriculum that can be labeled general courses. The courses students take within a chosen major, whether it be in arts and sciences or a preprofessional field, are in no way constrained, or even seriously addressed, by the ambitious goals for learning that faculty carefully identify through general education reviews. Acute observers question how serious such self-limiting exercises in educational planning can really be. As Leon Botstein (1991), a keen observer of the contemporary scene, remarks, "Institutions' struggles over cores, coherence, canons . . . result from an artificial triage. People are fighting over 10 percent of the territory while the remaining 90 percent appears untouchable" (p. 14).

This contemporary academic triage helps account for another curious anomaly in the national debate about purpose and practice in higher education. Though one would not know it from the increasingly acerbic public challenges being posed to higher education, reform initiatives are well advanced in the majority of U.S. colleges and universities. Campus-led calls for reform and recommendations for achieving it became widespread in the 1980s; by the end of that decade, hundreds of institutions had undertaken time-consuming and extensive educational reviews. Analyzing trends on 305 such campuses, Jerry Gaff (1991) reports that 42 percent of the deans responding to a survey described at least moderate change in their institutions' programs while another 42 percent described large changes (p. 76). With few exceptions, however, the reform initiatives reported by these deans conform to the pattern described earlier. Their institutions have defined overarching goals for all students' learning but address these goals through the fraction of the curriculum that meets general education requirements.

Reform activities of this kind have not assuaged higher education's critics, either on or off campus. Despite the enormous effort and energy that colleges and universities have undeniably expended on general education reviews and reforms over the past decade, attacks on the effectiveness of baccalaureate programs have, if anything, only increased in the 1990s. Discontent about the quality of U.S. undergraduate education remains palpable. On all sides, there are complaints that institutions' curricula lack purpose, focus, and coherence—and, therefore, accountability. There are widespread calls for new attention to—and new rewards for—effective college teaching. Educational assessment initiatives, mounted in nearly all states by 1990 and currently, as a consequence of federal mandate, required by all of the nation's regional accrediting associations, reflect this discontent. Many educational observers predict that the federally initiated standards-setting exercises now under way for the nation's public schools will eventually be extended to colleges and universities.

In his ambitious national study of the effects of college (conducted as part of an Exxon Educational Foundation effort to examine the effects of general education reform), Alexander Astin (1992) adds another dimension to the chorus of criticism. Studying more than 24,000 college students graduating in 1989, Astin found that only 38.8 percent thought their ability to think critically was "much stronger in 1989 than 1985," only 32.5 percent thought their analytical and problem-solving skills were much stronger, and only 27.6 percent considered their writing skills much stronger (p. 223). With critical thinking, analytical, problem-solving, and writing skills high on everyone's list of goals for baccalaureate education and stipulations for general education courses, these graduates' self-reports about the effect of college on their capabilities must give us pause. Moreover, it appears that the students were not unduly modest. King and Kitchener's discussion (Chapter Two) of students' development of reflective thinking in the college years provide telling evidence that students develop much less sophistication about the complex dimensions of thinking and judgment in college than either campus rhetoric or educators' best visions would suggest.

This juxtaposition of widespread and well-intentioned campus reform efforts with an increasingly insistent questioning of educational effectiveness should not surprise us. Deliberately self-limiting reforms should be expected to have, in the end, limited effects. Although general education reviews have served a salutary purpose on most campuses that initiated them, general education courses cannot be expected to bear, by themselves, the whole burden of improving the quality of college students' learning. Astin's study of college student outcomes directly challenges the disparity between the energy faculty are addressing to general education reform and that reform's limited effect on student learning. As Astin crisply reports, despite all the attention given to general education curricula in the past decade, the actual structure of the general education program at most institutions seems to have had no discernible effects on a wide variety of outcomes frequently identified as valued goals of general education (p. 424). For the 90 percent of general education programs that meet their general education goals through some version of a distributional system, "what specific options are offered, how much freedom of choice is allowed, and whether particular types of courses are required does not appear to have any substantial effect on how students develop during their undergraduate years. To a certain extent, this suggests that we may be spinning our wheels when we devote so much faculty time and energy to discussions and debates about the content and form of general education" (p. 425).

The Need for a New Approach

For students and faculty members alike, the heart of a curriculum is the work undertaken in departments, the specialized focused study in what we conventionally call majors, major programs, or concentrations. Yet by tacit common compact, effective throughout the United States, the educational strategies of major programs are exempted from curricular committees' review. While many institutions have established procedures for departmental program reviews, typically these reviews are a combination of a departmental audit and a strategic plan for helping departments remain current with new scholarship. Rarely do such reviews focus on the educational coherence and effectiveness of the programs of study offered as departmental majors. Even more rarely do they proceed within a framework of shared institutional assumptions about how work undertaken within a major program is expected to contribute to an institution's carefully articulated, overarching goals for all students' learning. Both the work of the major and the work of general education are undermined by these artificial divisions between the different parts of students' educational experiences in college.

In the pages that follow, the authors of this volume argue that, if we seriously wish to strengthen the practice and effectiveness of baccalaureate studies in U.S. colleges and universities, we need to address the quality of students' learning within the major. If we want students to more fully develop the knowledge and intellectual capacities that prepare them to live and work in the contemporary world, we must ask that each major provide a cognitive apprenticeship that fosters students' acquisition of complex knowledge and advanced analytical capacities. Faculty in each department need to look at the educational expectations and practices of their major programs in relation to their institution's overarching goals for education; equally important, they need to look at the educational potential of connecting the major to general education and elective courses.

Institutional custom and departmental tradition have drawn firm lines between the major and the rest of the curriculum in our colleges and universities. However, students' minds should not be so compartmentalized. While it is impossible for most institutions to develop a coherent curriculum that could be offered as a common program for every student, it is not impossible for us to develop learning models that teach each student how to integrate the different parts of his or her chosen curriculum. It is both possible and desirable to establish connected knowing as a normative expectation for all students' learning, understanding that the integrative forms and strategies will vary for each student and each course of study. The work undertaken within a field should be purposeful, developmental, and cumulative; the work in general education and electives should—and can—provide an enriching critical dialogue with the work students take in a particular field. Students challenged to think more intensively and extensively about connecting knowledge from different parts of their studies and about the relationships among different ways of construing the world should be more likely to attest that their intellectual capacities are much stronger at graduation than they were at entrance. Even better, the students should be able to say how their capacities were developed through studies across a curriculum. Most importantly, they should leave college with a rich repertoire of usable capacities and intellectual strategies with which to engage new forms of learning and knowledge use outside the academy.

The Major and Goals for Liberal Learning

This volume is a resource for faculty members and academic administrators who care about the quality of their students' learning and want to improve it. Strongly challenging the traditions that exclude major programs from most discussions of ways to improve students' learning in college, the chapters that follow suggest that the major can be viewed as a matrix for liberal education, an organizing center that can and should help students develop both analytical competence and broad, integrated, contextual knowledge about their chosen field of study.

Two themes run through the volume. The first is a view of good education as integrating education. As we have mentioned, typically educators have emphasized the opposition between majors and general education—one viewed as specialized, perhaps too specialized; the other seen as broad and integrative. But there are other ways to conceive this relationship: specialized knowledge might be viewed as a framework or center for integrating, extending, and generalizing knowledge. This volume explores ways of framing the major as integrative and interdisciplinary learning.

The second theme is a commitment to educational community as a necessary dimension of higher education. The importance of this theme is increasingly supported by research. Astin's research (1992) points over-whelmingly to the importance of intellectual relationships with both peers and faculty as a context for intellectual and personal maturation in college. Uri Treisman's successful work (1992) with at-risk minority students studying cal-culus, and a host of related models for improving at-risk students' learning, further underline the close relationship between the quality of students' learn-ing and their participation in supportive learning communities. Vincent Tinto and others (1993), now studying the effects of collaborative learning commu-nities on students' persistence and achievement, add additional weight to the growing body of empirical evidence. Educational community is an integral dimension of collegial inquiry and achievement. In the traditional model of higher education, intellectual involvement with faculty and peers was sup-ported and facilitated by students' residence on campus. For today's college students, educational community is more difficult to find. The majority are nonresident, commuting to and from their home campuses, often working, fre-quently raising a family while also going to college. Many students who do live on campus attend huge universities where relationships built around academic work are often hard to establish. Reporting on studies of peer and faculty relationships at Harvard University, Richard Light observes that "nearly with-out exception, students who feel they have not yet found themselves, or fully hit their stride, report they have not developed such relationships" (1992, p. 8). If high-ability students (as we may assume the Harvard students are) require significant engagement with others for their intellectual development, so too do all our students, most especially those for whom college means com-ing to terms with assumptions and approaches very different from those encountered outside the college gates.

AAC's Work on Revitalizing Majors

This volume draws extensively on work initiated by the Association of Amer-ican Colleges (AAC)[1] in concert with a dozen learned societies and several col-leges and universities. Between 1988 and 1991, with support from the U.S. Department of Education Fund for the Improvement of Postsecondary Edu-cation and the Ford Foundation, AAC worked in collaboration with twelve learned societies to reexamine the educational goals for arts and sciences majors in the context of a baccalaureate degree. The reexamination had four emphases: a focus on students for whom the arts and sciences major is part of a broad liberal education rather than the first stage in professional training; an articulation of the educational goals, organizing principles, and enabling cur-ricular structures that would support students' intellectual development through studies in the major; an examination of ways to connect students' learning in the major with other parts of their learning; and the encouragement of faculties' collegial responsibility for the integrity and vitality of major pro-grams. This initiative, which led to a series of national reports on the major

(Association of American Colleges, 1991a, 1991b, 1992), is described in detail in Chapter Four. The AAC recommendations also form a framework for this volume as it explores both the analyses behind the recommendations and the implications for campus practice.

Like the AAC study, this volume focuses on arts and sciences majors as contexts for liberal learning. In the conventional wisdom of U.S. higher education, liberal learning and a major in an arts and sciences field are often assumed to be synonymous. However, if we want to understand normatively, rather than conventionally, what establishes work in a major as liberal rather than preprofessional, we need to begin by querying goals, practices, and educational ethos in those fields that deliberately embrace liberal education as their mission. This volume's exploration of the arts and sciences major as liberalizing is not, however, simply inductive. It argues that arts and sciences majors must adopt new norms and new, self-reflexive standards if they are to fulfill their espoused commitment to liberal learning in practice.

Yet this volume also reaches beyond arts and sciences, or disciplinary, majors. The great majority of U.S. college students elect preprofessional rather than arts and sciences majors. If the artificial boundary that now divides considerations of learning in general education from considerations of learning in a major is a general problem in higher education, it is an especially pernicious problem for those students who study preprofessional subjects. In principle, if too rarely in practice, preprofessional studies can be significantly enhanced by the integration of content and critical perspectives drawn from liberal arts fields. Business majors should be able to locate their work in the history of industrialization; majors in virtually any field from physics to history to engineering need to know in depth the culture and history of other parts of the world and at least one foreign language. As we learn what counts as liberal learning in arts and sciences majors, we will find principles that apply to students' learning in any focused major, whether it be literature or education, biology or accounting.

This volume is divided into three parts. Part One (Chapters One to Three) raises a series of pointed questions about the effectiveness of the major in fostering one of the most commonly valued outcomes of a liberal education: competence in analysis, argument, and reflective thinking. In Chapter One, Jonathan Z. Smith severely critiques the quality of students' learning in arts and sciences fields, challenging the conventional wisdom that these majors effectively provide a reflective education distinctively different in quality from that encountered in professional studies. Chapter Two, by Patricia M. King and Karen Strohm Kitchener, provides evidence that college study in general falls signally short in providing students either understanding of what it means to make an argument or competence in what the authors call reflective thinking. In Chapter Three, Carol Geary Schneider draws on the critique presented in Chapters One and Two to ask whether there remains a compelling rationale for study in a specific field.

Part Two (Chapters Four and Five) discusses the AAC framework for revitalizing majors. In Chapter Four, Carol Geary Schneider describes the set of organizing principles proposed by AAC's national study group to guide students' development of analytical capacities, integrative learning, and critical perspectives. In Chapter Five, Joan S. Stark and Lisa R. Lattuca look at different fields' response to these organizing principles and the principles' capacity to guide liberal learning in a broad range of humanities, social sciences, and scientific fields.

The authors of Part Three (Chapters Six and Seven) look at the major as a community for teaching and learning and at the responsibilities that follow from that view. Chapter Six, by Elaine P. Maimon, examines the major as a "home" or supportive context for students' explorations; Chapter Seven, by William Scott Green, explores the major as a teaching and learning collective that imparts to students the skills in research and teaching that faculty members themselves use as modes of learning.

If the pages that follow offer one lesson, it is this: educators must come to terms both with the reality of the knowledge explosion in our time and with the cogency of the revised epistemological concepts now also exploding in virtually every field. We can no longer define education through a particular major solely in terms of information that every student in the field must acquire. Nor can we assume certainty about the standing of the concepts and information students do acquire. Concepts are refined; information is revised, challenged, discarded; significance varies depending on the point of view of the interpreter. All these factors point to the importance of community in both knowing and thinking. If education for the twenty-first century is to provide students with critical skills and a framework for continuing learning, it must help them grasp the role of communities in developing and authorizing knowledge, and it must give them practice in querying the claims of any community to final knowledge.

This is the challenge of liberal education in our time—and it is a challenge we must assign to every major.

Carol Geary Schneider
William Scott Green
Editors

Note

1. The Association of American Colleges will soon change its name to The Association of American Colleges and Universities.

References

Association of American Colleges. Liberal Learning and the Arts and Sciences Major. Vol. 1: The Challenge of Connecting Learning. Washington, D.C.: Association of American Colleges, 1991a.
Association of American Colleges. Liberal Learning and the Arts and Sciences Major. Vol. 2: Reports from the Fields. Washington, D.C.: Association of American Colleges, 1991b.

Association of American Colleges. *Liberal Learning and the Arts and Sciences Major*. Vol. 3: *Program Review and Educational Quality in the Major*. Washington, D.C.: Association of American Colleges, 1992.

Astin, A. W. *What Matters in College? Four Critical Years Revisited*. San Francisco: Jossey-Bass, 1992.

Botstein, L. "Structuring Specialization as a Form of General Education." *Liberal Education*, 1991, 77 (2), 10–19.

Gaff, J. G. *New Life for the College Curriculum: Assessing Achievements and Furthering Progress in the Reform of General Education*. San Francisco: Jossey-Bass, 1991.

Kimball, B. *Orators and Philosophers: A History of the Idea of Liberal Education*. New York: Teachers College Press, 1986.

Light, R. *Explorations with Students and Faculty About Teaching, Learning, and Student Life*. The Harvard Assessment Seminars, Second Report, 1992.

Tinto, V., and others. "Building Community Among New College Students." *Liberal Education*, 1993, 79 (4).

Treisman, U. "Studying Students Studying Calculus: A Look at the Lives of Minority Mathematics Students in College." *College Mathematics Journal*, 1992, 23 (5), 362–372.

CAROL GEARY SCHNEIDER is executive vice president of the Association of American Colleges and director of AAC's initiatives on revitalizing majors.

WILLIAM SCOTT GREEN is professor of religion, Philip S. Bernstein Professor of Judaic Studies, and dean of undergraduate studies, College of Arts and Science, University of Rochester.

PART ONE

Arts and Sciences Majors:
A Critical Assessment

Students must learn the subject matter and conventions of their majors but must also become part of a larger knowledge community in order to understand disciplinary processes and conventions from a broader perspective. Educators must take responsibility for helping students accomplish both these goals.

To Double Business Bound

Jonathan Z. Smith

As a college instructor, I have worried for years about the problems of teaching modes of active reading. One simple device I have used is to ask students to keep a journal-like set of notes in which they record their guesses, their questions, their comparisons between texts, and so forth, and to review these notes with them (along with the underlining in their texts) in individual conferences fairly early on in a course. I have just finished a 7:00 a.m. to 6:00 p.m. week of such meetings with students in my year-long course on Religion in Western Civilization. In particular, I think of two students whose comments, made in passing, and taken together, would more than satiate any structuralist's lust for opposition and inversion. One was a student in the physical sciences; the other, a major in one of the social sciences.

The first student had his appointment with me shortly after a physics class. He complained that, contrary to his expectations, in the "hard sciences" (his term) nothing was definite. Matters he had laboriously mastered in high school were constantly being dismissed in college ("we no longer think that that is the case"), and he suspected that this would continue at each level of learning. He responded with depression to the same situation that Martin Gardner is said to have reported with enthusiasm some thirty years ago: A student at the Institute for Advanced Studies in Princeton was asked how his seminar had been that day. He was quoted as exclaiming, "Wonderful! Everything we knew about physics last week isn't true!" My student had come into my religion class in the belief that matters would be more certain there, that religion had secure knowledge. (He admitted that he found what we were doing in class just as depressing as his physics class.) The social sciences student had the opposite problem. As we reviewed her notebook together, she repeatedly insisted, "It's all bull." "Everything is interpretation." "You just deal with words, you have no facts."

NEW DIRECTIONS FOR HIGHER EDUCATION, no. 84, Winter 1993 © Jossey-Bass Publishers

Both of these students are seniors. Both have been good students although not outstanding. Both are expecting to undertake postbaccalaureate studies.

If they appear to us to be naive—the physical science student with his odd nostalgia for the human sciences as the realm of unchanging truth and values, the social science student with her equally odd nostalgia for the physical sciences as a realm of fact and certainty—to whose account should this be charged? To the students'? Or to that of the education they have received? Neither student, despite the ten or twelve courses each has taken in his or her major program, has an adequate understanding of an academic discipline. The fault is surely ours, not theirs.

Interpretive Communities

At other times, and in other contexts, I might have used such an anecdote to introduce my longstanding suspicion of the major: that it is, at best, an inadequate mode of education given its stated goals; that it is, more usually, pernicious. But that will not be my tack here. Rather, I will stipulate the presence of something like the major as a means of focusing education with its notion of "interpretive communities" or "knowledge communities," in order to raise some reformist or revisionist notions.

At the outset, we need to pause and be attentive to words. After all, the social science student was right. By and large, we academicians do deal with words. But rather than weakening us, as she thought, words are what empower us for good or ill—empower us with respect to the world, to other folk, and to one another within the academy. Anyone who doubts this need only turn to any number of works of feminist criticism, the most powerful and fundamental internal critique of the academy since Kant.

I like the terms *interpretive communities,* or *discourse communities.* I think I like them even better than the word *disciplines,* which they are, in part, intended to replace. While *discipline* contains the notion of instruction and learning, it is the passive rather than the active sense that is to the fore, as its root *dek* (to accept) and the use of *discipline* as a transitive verb signify, and as its cognates *disciple, dogma,* and *docile* make plain. *Community* evokes a quite different politics. It carries the root connotation of exchange rather than subjugation. It suggests notions of common goods, reciprocity, and communication. Disciplines have students (that is, disciples); communities have colleagues. You can learn discipline; you must participate in a community.

Such lexicographical games are suggestive without necessarily having to bear the burden of being true. Indeed, when we look at a sophisticated definition of discipline, we find a far more social connotation than the word may, at first glance, seem to imply. The most thoughtful definition of discipline that I know appears in the first volume of Stephen Toulmin's masterwork, *Human*

Understanding: "A collective human enterprise takes the form of a rationally developing 'discipline' in those cases where . . . [a] shared commitment to a sufficiently agreed set of ideals leads to the development of an isolable and self-defining repertory of procedures; and where those procedures are open to further modification so as to deal with problems arising from the incomplete fulfillment of those disciplinary ideals" (1972, p. 359). Note the central argument. For Toulmin, well-formed disciplines are constituted "not by the types of objects with which they deal [their subject matters], but rather by the questions which arise about them [their goals]" (p. 149). The distinctive mark of a discipline is that these questions represent a shared commitment, a sufficient agreement, a collective enterprise (p. 359). Disciplines are not given; they are not determined by what is out there. Rather, they are the result of a social compact, a covenant. It is their corporate "ideals" and goals—their projections rather than their achievements—that mark off disciplines from pseudo-disciplines and that distinguish one discipline from another.

This leads Toulmin to argue that continuity in a discipline is to be sought neither in the history of its so-called triumphs, its answers (the all-too-common banal and misleading mode of presenting the history of science), nor "in any single unchanging question or group of questions" (the equally common, banal, and misleading way of presenting the history of the human sciences, such as philosophy), but in what he terms the "continuing genealogy of problems" (p. 148). Problems, as Toulmin understands them, are caused by the gap between a discipline's "ideals" and its "current capacities" (p. 152). This gap generates "the isolable and self-defining repertory of procedures" characteristic of a given discipline. If I may be allowed, by way of an aside, to put this in my sort of language (with only rough congruence to Toulmin's), we choose a disciplinary stance—or perhaps more pointedly, at the subdisciplinary level, a theoretical or methodological posture—not by its successes so much as by the problems we are willing to live with. As a historian in the field of religion, I would rather go to bed at night with the headaches that position necessarily leads to than with the headaches entailed by the phenomenological approach of some of my colleagues. Because of the inescapable gap, disciplinary choice is as much, if not more, an index of pain than of pleasure.

Let's return to Toulmin. He uses a variety of languages to underscore the essentially social nature of his understanding of discipline. He writes that one must become an "heir" to the genealogy of problems (p. 146, n. 1). Elsewhere, he asserts that "the one indispensable step in any [disciplinary] apprenticeship" is "to enter imaginatively" into the discipline's "intellectual ideals" (p. 153). At another point, he insists that there are "collective ambitions" one "commits" oneself to when one "enrolls" in the profession that corresponds to a given discipline (p. 154). Finally, he affirms that a discipline is transmitted from one generation to another "by a process of enculturation" (p. 159). Taken together, these sentences add up to an implicit theory and model of education.

I shall not tease out the lineaments of this model, for there is a rub. Toulmin's definition of discipline as I quoted it began with a limiting clause that I have thus far ignored: "a collective human enterprise takes the form of a *rationally developing* discipline *in those cases* . . . " (p. 359). Elsewhere, Toulmin limits his definition by referring to "a compact discipline" (p. 379). Such limiting terms will give neither aid nor comfort to anyone who would seek to identify the heterogenous items that make up the present map of collegiate and curricular organization with Toulmin's understanding of discipline. The majority of motley subject areas that we politically recognize as fields or disciplines in our curricula fail at almost every point to fulfill Toulmin's definition of a "compact" and a "rationally developing" discipline. At best, they might be classified under the rubrics Toulmin develops towards the end of his work: "diffuse disciplines," "would-be disciplines," and "non-disciplinary intellectual activities" (pp. 378–411). In some instances, what our curricula do escapes even these generously flabby characterizations.

There is yet another issue. Toulmin's discussion requires that disciplines always be seen in relation to notions of professions and professionalism. To the degree that we continue to perceive liberal learning as distinct from preprofessional training (a distinction that is problematic), then the ethical question arises: Ought we to be engaged in enculturating college students into the several disciplines? Or, to put the matter more pragmatically: Should we continue to do the work of graduate education in college? I would want to insist that, to either form of the question, the answer is no. It would be a separate argument to demonstrate that graduate education, more often than not, fails at achieving its legitimate educational goals, but that argument can be suggested by rephrasing the question: Why should college teachers continue to do worse at what graduate faculties already do badly?

Having looked briefly at the language of the disciplines, we need to return to the nomenclature *knowledge communities*, a suggestive term of uncertain pedigree. I confess that I was not helped much in thinking about the implications of this terminological shift by any number of readings, and therefore, I turn for clarification to the gemeinschaft/gesellschaft literature of social theory (with all its well-known problems) and, in particular, the classic work of Robert MacIver (1970). MacIver understood *community* to be a relative term. Nevertheless, he argued, it can be characterized "in some kind and degree [by] distinctive common characteristics—manners, traditions, modes of speech, and so on" (p. 30). To this notion of community, he contrasted the *association*, which was "an organization of social beings (or a body of social beings as organized) for the pursuit of some common interest or interests. It is a determinate social unity built upon common purpose" (p. 30). He went on to suggest that associations can be classified by their types of interests (for example, whether unspecialized or specialized) and the relative duration of their interests, from "temporary" and "realizable once for all" to "interests unlimited by a time-span" (pp. 56–59). I would add that associations, or organizations, are subgroups within a community (or can link subgroups across communities). While community usually implies singularity, organizations are more readily plural—a single individual can have simultaneous multiple memberships in a variety of organizations reflecting a plurality of interests. Finally, while communities strive for unity by encompassing diversity, organizations are frequently characterized by what anthropologists call segmentation. That is to say, when an organization reaches a certain, often demographic, limit, it splits. There is symmetrical balance and opposition between segments and unified resistance among all the segments to any superordinate entity.

I put this in terms of the present issue, and, mindful of a partial parallel to Toulmin's characterization of discipline, we might formulate matters in the following manner: the academy (as exemplified in a college or university) is a community; the several disciplines are organizations, usually oriented towards specialized goals of unlimited duration. Academic departments, which may or may not be coextensive with disciplines, serve as organizations that exhibit all the segmentary politics described by anthropologists: segmentation for largely demographic reasons, balanced opposition among themselves, and unitary resistance to a superordinate entity, usually the college or university as a whole.

Introductory Tasks

What have I gained by this sort of playful linguistic sleight-of-hand? At the very least, it reminds us of something that the language of knowledge communities tempts us to fudge: there are two distinct introductory tasks that we confront as educators. The first is the introduction, the initiation, the enculturation of our students into the community of the college as different from the communities they know best, most particularly the world of home and of secondary schooling. The former we tend to address largely through the extra curriculum, ranging from residence (in some institutions) to diversity in admissions (in most). Curricularly, we address these issues only obliquely, by challenging students' notions of the authority of tradition, by instilling an ethic of everything, at least in principle, being open to suspicion and question. By largely confining the contrast between the college and home communities to the extracurricular, faculties have remained often unconscious of, indeed, blasè toward this most central, and often most painful, process of enculturation.

The students' second introduction, the initiation into the difference between the community of high school and that of college, especially with respect to work (a difference that, above all else, ought to be one of the most explicit objects of reflection in higher education) is chiefly seen as a matter of general education and, more recently, of programs in generic skills such as writing and critical reasoning. For central to this difference between communities is a change in attitude toward words and discourse. In college-level work, words are rarely thought to be expressive of things (in philosophical terms, they are no longer held to be "real"), they are no longer vocabularies to be mastered (30 Minutes A Day), or to be judged by the degree to which they conform to something "out there." In a college community, it is we who master words. Rather than evaluate the relationship of words to things, we evaluate the relationship of words to other words and to other acts of human imagination. It is a process that has many names; above all it is known as argumentation. For it is argument which marks the distinctive mode of speech which characterizes the college community.

There is latent in such a conception of the tasks of general education (when it is not reduced, in a core program or the like, to some notion of common acquaintance with a specific body of texts or concepts) a set of issues that have yet to be addressed widely by the educational community. Such matters have been raised in polemic works such as *Critical Thinking and Education* (McPeck, 1981) as well as by some of the newer studies in rhetoric and by linguistic research in such fields as performance-theory and pragmatics. Common to all these is suspicion of the notion of a universal audience and, therefore, a denial of the plausibility of generic argument and omnipurpose, omnicompetent writing capacities.

Disciplinary Barriers

To return to MacIver's characterizations, while it may be the case that the academy as a community can be distinguished from other communities by its modes of speech, the various organizations within the academy, because of their separate goals, may differ from one another even more widely. Allow me to quote three statements in illustration of this difference.

The first, taken from Gilbert Ryle's attack on the adequacy of universal notions of formal logic, points out that "a first-rate mathematician and a first-rate literary critic might share the one intellectual virtue of arguing impeccably, while their other intellectual virtues could be so disparate that neither could cope even puerilely with the problems of the other. Each thinks scrupulously inside his own field, but most of their scruples are of entirely different kinds" (1962, p. 21). The second statement is McPeck's bold assertion that "there are as many types of legitimate argument as there are fields or subjects that may be argued about. . . . And fields, with their corresponding modes of reasoning, differ more widely than species of animals" (1981, p. 79). While perhaps somewhat hyperbolic, his statement incarnates one of my old professors' definition of a scholarly theory: "an exaggeration in the direction of the truth" (McPeck, 1981).

The third example is the most telling, for the author, the late Nobel prize-winning physicist Richard Feynman, is innocent of any theoretical or educational purpose in reporting his anecdote. He writes that he decided to spend his summer vacations not by traveling to a different place but by studying in a different field. One summer and one sabbatical year were spent working on bacteriophages and doing other experiments in the biology laboratories at the California Institute of Technology. According to his report, his results were significant enough to interest James Watson and to have Feynman himself invited to give a set of seminars to biologists at Harvard. Nevertheless, he says:

> [The] work on phage I never wrote up. . . . I did write something informally on it. I sent it to [Bob] Edgar [who was in charge of the biology lab], who laughed when he read it. It wasn't in the standard form that biologists use—first procedures, and so forth. I spent a lot of time explaining things that all the biologists knew. Edgar made a shortened version, but I couldn't understand it. I don't think they ever published it. . . . I learned a lot of things in biology. . . . I got better at pronouncing the words, knowing what not to include in a paper or a seminar, and detecting a weak technique in an experiment. But I love physics, and I love to go back to it [Feynman, 1984, pp. 72–73].

Just how complex a matter Feynman signals with the phrase "it wasn't in the standard form that biologists use" may be illustrated by a number of careful studies, most especially the work of Knorr-Cetina (1981) that traces the development of a scientific research paper from the original experiment and lab notebook through all the intermediary draftings and revisions to the final published form.

Reflecting on these three examples produces any number of educational implications. The statements suggest, among other matters, that it may well be particular knowledge communities that ought to take chief responsibility for college-level writing, rather than programs in generic expository writing aimed at an abstract and universalized audience. Conversely, one might conclude that other modes of writing—especially more reflexive styles and genres, such as letters or journals—ought to be to the fore in general education courses as being particularly appropriate to these courses' task of enculturating the student into the academic community at large.

Feynman's anecdote allows us, as well, to begin to specify responsibilities implicit in the introductory role of the several knowledge communities, responsibilities that must gain explicit recognition in the communities' curricula, educational procedures, and objectives. Abstracting Feynman's themes, we can construct a rudimentary mini-curriculum for enculturating students into a given knowledge community. First, they need to learn something of the domain, or the topics, of the knowledge community, especially as expressed in the jargon of the field (compare Feynman's comment about getting "better at pronouncing the words"). Second, and even more important in many respects than becoming articulate in the field, is the contrary skill of mastering the repression of speech, learning the tacit conventions, the matters stipulated or taken for granted, which do not have to be said. (In Feynman's terms, the experience of "explaining things that all the biologists know"). Third, students must learn what counts as appropriate according to the conventions of the field (as Feynman learned how to detect "weak technique" and Ryle noted indigenous "scruples"). And fourth, students must become adept in the necessarily fictive modes of accepted disciplinary discourse. (This skill, suggested by Feynman's learning "what not to include in a paper or seminar," is raised to a procedural principle by the distinguished biologist Peter Medawar in his oft-cited observation that the conventions of the biological research paper not only "conceal but actively misrepresent" what occurs in the laboratory (1969, p. 69).

Note the stunning results when these four tasks (and there are, of course, others) are not made an explicit part of a curriculum and an enculturation process. A Nobel laureate in physics is laughed at by his biologist colleagues when he writes up his biological experiments. Conversely, when a professional biologist writes up Feynman's experiments and results "in the standard form," Feynman cannot understand the result. How much more are such consequences compounded at the collegiate level, where the initiate is not a Nobel laureate but rather a neophyte or, God help us, a student from one knowledge community fulfilling a requirement in another community's course? By and large, it is only the first task, the "pronunciation of words," that is routinely and explicitly addressed. The other items, from which the faculty largely abstains, are left to the student's initiative (and failure), to his or her capacities for observation, for intuition, for mimesis—the same methods of learning, I would note, by which planaria become able to negotiate a maze.

Necessary Duplicities

It is at this point that we may fruitfully rejoin the two students with whom I began: the student in the physical sciences for whom surety gained at one stage of education was rudely overthrown at another, an individual who might be characterized as given to premature certainty, and the student in the social sciences for whom all was opinion and nothing secure, an individual who might be characterized as given to premature uncertainty. Neither of these students had been let in on educators' pedagogical secret: the necessary duplicity of what educators do. Each saw one or the other side of educators' efforts, but we educators are to double business bound.

In introducing a college student to what is usually termed a disciplinary framework, we have, at first, to disguise the problematic. We have to act and speak as if our informed guesses are more grounded in the way things are than is the case. Thus every course, regardless of format, functions as a survey. It teaches the student what words are important and how to pronounce them. The words, the objects displayed, are taken as if they were self-evidently significant. We conceal from our students the debates and uncertainties that lie behind such judgments—indeed, we largely conceal from them the fact that self-evidence is always a field-specific judgment. We traditionally screen from our students' view the hard work that results in the production of the exemplary texts, items, and problems on display—indeed, we treat these sources as found objects, hiding, for example, the immense editorial labors that conjecturally established so many of the texts routinely taken as classics (not to speak of the labors of translation), and read them with students as if each word were directly revelatory. In some courses, we also gloss over the history of failed experiments and sheer serendipity that underlies the laws and models we present to our students as inevitable. In enculturating courses, we treat theory as fact. Students in the humanities know that there is such a thing as an author's intention and regularly and effortlessly recover it. Students in the social sciences know that there is such a thing as a society that functions and regularly and effortlessly observe it. Students in the sciences are all (without knowing it) wedded to the philosophical tradition of induction that runs from Bacon to Mill and that, ironically, makes the students conceptually indistinguishable from Bible Belt creationists and fundamentalists.

Despite our claims to teach how and not what, as our students highlight their texts (call the texts in and look at them), it is the theoretical conclusions that they note with a yellow smear, not processes that do not lend themselves readily to such magic markings. And nothing we say or do in class, in assignments, or in examinations suggests that students should be otherwise engaged. In classroom discussion, as if at some afternoon television quiz show, they call out answers at one another and think they are discussing method.

The letter is reinforced by our laying on them the fake ethic of originality (one that is already inappropriate at the Ph.D. level and sheerly ludicrous at the collegiate). In this way, we cover up the teamwork, collegiality, and interdependence that underlie most research activities, and we leave students alone and separated from one another to cherish their personal conclusions, often unconscious of how they reached them and barred from making any procedural contrasts by means of examples, interrogations, challenges, or rival proposals from their fellow students. In a bizarre inversion, our structured forms of socialization into disciplinary communities result in onanism.

Second-Order Reflection

If, as I have suggested, all these concealments, all these acts of apparent bad faith, are justified pedagogically by the strategic necessity for duplicity at the beginning, if we must behave in such a manner and encourage our students to do likewise, then a dramaturge may properly ask, Where, then, is the peripeteia? Where is the turnabout? Where is the unmasking? At what point do we as teachers allow our students to experience what I would call the wink? Is it at some point during a course? Is it along the way of a four-year course of study? Is it a delayed payoff reserved only for those who go on to postbaccalaureate study? I am more certain that these sorts of questions are never asked by the majority of our faculties than I am of the answers. I am quite certain that most students never experience having the rug pulled out in a controlled way, never experience the gap that Toulmin argued was at the very center of a definition of discipline. I base this certainty on the fact that the curricula of most majors exhibit no dramatic structure. When they are not sheerly political (that is, students take a course with each professor), they are almost always constructed on the principle of more-of-the-same.

If we intend to continue the use of something like the major as the chief means of enculturation into a knowledge community in college, then faculty discussions of sequences, prerequisites, requirements, and certification will have to concern themselves largely with second-order reflections and discourse about such disciplinary concerns and become less preoccupied with first-order discourse concerning content. If faculty discussions do not do this, dramatic duplicity will have shaded over into fraud. Barring such discourse within the several organizations (that is, the departments), each institution as a whole (the community) will have to provide curricular time and space for students to reflect on their education in a way that the segmented faculty refuse to undertake. Either way, we need to think hard about final moments—projects or occasions for students toward the end of their collegiate experiences—that are not merely more-of-the-same-only-longer but that provide a significant and, in some sense, public occasion for reflexivity.

Anthropologists employ the term *joking relationships* to describe a mode of social interaction between intimates. I would hope for no better model of the sort of dramatic, yet comfortable, relationship that ought to obtain between faculty and students, students and students, and faculty and students and their modes of disciplinary attention. Jokes, as any reader of Freud's masterwork will testify, are fundamentally untranslatable because they are always insiders' speech. Enculturation is achieved when the outsider becomes, to some degree, an insider.

It is time we let one another and, above all, it is time we let our students in on the joke, taking *joke* in the sense stipulated by a recent social theorist: "A joke is a play on form. It brings into relation disparate elements in such a way that one accepted pattern is challenged by another. . . . [The joke] affords the opportunity for realizing that an accepted pattern has no necessity" (Douglas, 1968, p. 365). When all is said, disciplinary knowledge is this sort of joke and needs, for that very reason, to be taken seriously.

References

Douglas, M. "The Social Control of Cognition: Some Factors in Joke Perception." *Man,* 1968, *3,* 361–376.

Feynman, R. P. *"Surely You're Joking, Mr. Feynman."* New York: Norton, 1986.

Knorr-Cetina, K. D. *The Manufacture of Knowledge: An Essay on the Constructivist and Contextual Nature of Science.* Elmsford, N.Y.: Pergamon Press, 1981.

MacIver, R. M. *On Community, Society and Power.* Chicago: University of Chicago Press, 1970.

McPeck, J. *Critical Thinking and Education.* New York: St. Martin's Press, 1981.

Medawar, P. *The Art of the Soluble.* New York: Viking Penguin, 1969.

Ryle, G. *A Rational Animal.* London: Athlone Press, 1962.

Toulmin, S. E. *Human Understanding.* Vol. 1. Princeton, N.J.: Princeton University Press, 1972.

JONATHAN Z. SMITH is the Robert O. Anderson Distinguished Service Professor of the Humanities at the University of Chicago and coauthor of the Association of American Colleges reports Integrity in the College Curriculum *(1985) and* The Challenge of Connected Learning *(1991).*

This chapter describes evidence on how college students become increasingly able to reason about complex problems and discusses its implications for strengthening teaching and learning in the major.

The Development of Reflective Thinking in the College Years: The Mixed Results

Patricia M. King, Karen Strohm Kitchener

> Basically, you learn two kinds of things in college: *Things you will need to know in later life (2 hours)* . . . and *Things you will not need to know in later life (1198 hours).* These are the things you learn in classes whose names end in "ology," "osophy," "istry," "ics," and so on. The idea is, you memorize these things, then write them down in little exam books, then forget them. If you fail to forget them, you become a professor and have to stay in college for the rest of your life.
>
> —Dave Barry, 1981

This monograph on reforming the liberal arts major is intended to help faculty and academic administrators articulate fully and coherently what students should be expected to accomplish in the course of liberal learning. It also suggests ways that curricular practices can be intentionally designed to facilitate the achievement of these learning goals. At a time when there is much skepticism about the espoused benefits of participation in institutions of higher learning, there is greater urgency not only to clarify intended student outcomes, but to help more students achieve these goals. One intended outcome, perhaps the most common one, is the development of thinking skills. The benefits of attaining and honing both higher-order thinking skills and a disposition toward reflective thinking seem self-evident to most faculty and staff. However, these benefits and the role of the major are not always so clear to college students or even to college graduates. The humorous but cynical advice of Dave Barry (the syndicated columnist) to college students may reflect some of the real confusion about the goals of higher education and their relationship to the major. He said:

> After you've been in college for a year or so, you're supposed to choose a major, which is the subject you intend to memorize and forget the most things about. Here is a very important piece of advice: *Be sure to choose a major that does not involve Known Facts and Right Answers.*
>
> This means you must *not* major in mathematics, physics, biology, or chemistry, because these subjects involve actual facts. If, for example, you major in mathematics, you're going to wander into class one day and the professor will say: "Define the cosine integer of the quadrant of a rhomboid binary axis, and extrapolate your result to five significant vertices." If you don't come up with *exactly* the answer the professor has in mind, you fail. The same is true of chemistry: If you write in your exam book that carbon and hydrogen combine to form oak, your professor will flunk you. He wants you to come up with the same answer he and all the other chemists have agreed on. Scientists are extremely snotty about this.
>
> So you should major in subjects like English, philosophy, psychology, and sociology—subjects in which nobody really understands what anybody else is talking about, and which involve virtually no actual facts. (Barry, 1981)

Unfortunately, the perception that some majors involve "real facts" while others involve "just opinions" is one many college students hold. A few years ago, the authors of this chapter interviewed undergraduate science students about their choice of major and about classes in the humanities and social sciences. In explaining the differences, one student said he preferred the sciences because there the facts were clearer: "I mean, a bird has two feet; that's pretty conclusive."

The Association of American Colleges (AAC) study of arts and sciences majors, *The Challenge of Connecting Learning* (1991), also notes the emphasis in some majors on memorization of factual information: "The problem with the major is not that it has failed to deliver certain kinds of knowledge. The problem is that it often delivers too much knowledge with too little attention to how that knowledge is being created, what methods and modes of inquiry are employed in its creation, what presuppositions inform it, and what entailments flow from its particular ways of knowing, and between what students have learned and their lives beyond the academy" (p. 6). In other words, educators often treat a major simply as a body of knowledge, ignoring the mode of inquiry it also represents. The AAC report goes on to suggest that, in contrast, "the real challenge of college, for students and faculty members alike, is empowering individuals to know that the world is far more complex than it first appears, and that they must make interpretive arguments and decisions—judgments that entail real consequences for which they must take responsibility and from which they may not flee by disclaiming expertise" (pp. 16–17).

Educators have the responsibility to develop these interpretive abilities in students. To realize this ambitious educational goal, faculty must actively strive to learn more about students and to hone their own skills in responsibly assisting students to make interpretive arguments. In Chapter One, Jonathan Smith suggests that current teaching practices defeat these goals. This chapter examines the effectiveness of college programs from another vantage point, focusing on the authors' findings over the last fifteen years about the development of college students' reflective thinking abilities, especially their ability to reason effectively about complex problems. We hope that our findings, as well as the theoretical model in which they are grounded, will help faculty responsible for major programs understand how they can assist their students to rise to "the real challenge of college" by teaching them to make interpretive judgments in responsible, defensible ways. Our description of how students' thinking abilities develop is grounded in our research on the reflective judgment model of intellectual development (Kitchener and King, 1981; King and Kitchener, 1994). We have used this model and its research base to identify a variety of pedagogical and curricular issues associated with beginning, middle, and advanced courses in the major. In this chapter, we present the research on college students based on this model and then reflect on that research's implications for connecting learning in the major.

Different Problems Require Different Critical Thinking Skills

Thinking critically is a major hallmark of an educated person. It may also be the attribute that appears most frequently in both college mission statements and in lists of desirable attributes of an educated person (Bowen, 1977; Pascarella and Terenzini, 1991; Weingartner, 1991). Despite its centrality as an intended outcome of higher education, there is little consensus on what thinking critically actually is and even less consensus on how to teach students the habits of mind associated with thoughtful, reasoned judgments.

Much of the investigation of critical thinking has been directed toward logical reasoning, scientific reasoning, and the use of formal logic (Facione, 1990; Kurfiss, 1988). This work has been especially useful for understanding deductive reasoning, that is, how people reason about what Churchman (1971) calls "well-structured" problems or puzzles. Problems that can be solved with deductive logic can be described with a high degree of completeness, and problem solvers can be fairly certain that if they use the appropriate method or algorithm, the solution will be recognized and verified as correct. Examples of such well-structured problems include balancing a chemical equation or a checkbook, calculating interest payments on a business loan to be paid back over different periods of time, converting English measures to their metric equivalents, converting the cost of purchases made in one monetary system to the equivalent cost in another system, and calculating the correct trajectory for placing a satellite into a desired orbit. Even well-structured problems that are complex, difficult, and important can ultimately be solved with a high degree of certainty.

However, well-structured problems are not the only ones that require critical thinking, and other types of problems are not so amenable to correct and verifiable solutions. For example, the problems of evaluating alternative proposals to stimulate the economy or to reduce the deficit, weighing competing interpretations of national or international political events, and deciding whether the greenhouse effect will cause major climatic changes are not well defined. When addressing such problems, individuals may not have the complete information that would allow them to solve the problems with a high degree of certainty; they may not know what solutions are available or be able to adequately predict or evaluate the implications resulting from those solutions. And even when a solution is proposed, it is often hard to tell whether that solution would, in fact, resolve the problem.

These vexing problems are "ill-structured" (Churchman, 1971); they require what John Dewey (1933) referred to as a "reflective judgment." Reflective judgment, as Dewey understood it and as we use it in this chapter, is a grounded assertion, substantiated by valid reasoning, about a problematic situation. Dewey saw such judgment as the outcome of good thinking about problems that are uncertain of solution. This is the type of judgment we think the authors of The Challenge of Connecting Learning had in mind when they asserted that "students need to learn, through the kind of extended and direct experience afforded by concentrated studies, to be able to state why a question or argument is significant and for whom; what the difference is between developing and justifying a position and merely asserting one; and how to develop and provide warrants for their own interpretations and judgments" (Association of American Colleges, 1991, p. 14). While learning to reason well about both well- and ill-structured problems is an important attribute of an educated person, it should be noted that different educational goals are associated with the two objects of critical thinking (King and Kitchener, 1994). For well-structured problems, the educational goal is the ability to reason to correct solutions. For ill-structured problems, the goal is the ability to construct and defend reasonable solutions, a goal that is clearly reflected in the material we have already quoted from The Challenge of Connecting Learning.

How does the ability to construct reasonable solutions develop? This question has been the focus of our research on reflective judgment. Our Reflective Judgment Model can help college educators understand how they can use educationally sound strategies to help students to question assumptions about knowing and learning and to make more reasoned, defensible judgments. The model can also help those concerned with reforming the liberal arts major consider how different disciplines can contribute to the development of students' abilities to reason about ill-structured problems.

The Reflective Judgment Model

To develop the Reflective Judgment Model, we first asked people at a variety of educational levels to discuss four ill-structured problems in the intellectual domain: how the Egyptian pyramids were built, the safety of chemical additives in foods, how we as people came to be (did we evolve?), and objectivity in news reporting. We then asked a series of questions designed to elicit the basis of each person's point of view, the certainty with which that view was held, how the person evaluated the adequacy of alternative interpretations, and how she or he understood differences in perspectives and opinions. Based on the responses given during these Reflective Judgment Interviews, we identified seven sets of assumptions about knowledge and knowing and seven corresponding concepts of justification. This ordered set of assumptions and concepts became the Reflective Judgment Model. Its seven stages reflect individuals' development from pre-reflective to reflective thinking. (The following summary of the model is based on King and Kitchener, 1994. For more thorough descriptions of the stages of reflective judgment, see King and Kitchener, 1994; Kitchener, King, Wood, and Davison, 1989.)

Pre-Reflective Thinking. The Reflective Judgment Model describes a progression from pre-reflective to reflective thinking. In stages 1, 2, and 3, individuals generally hold the assumption that knowledge is gained either by direct, personal observation or through the word of an authority figure (see Figures 2.1, 2.2, 2.3). People who hold the assumptions associated with these stages are unable to differentiate between well- and ill-structured problems, viewing all problems as if they were well-structured. In other words, they assume all problems are completely defined and can be answered with certainty. We call thinking characterized by these assumptions pre-reflective thinking. This thinking is most typical of junior high and high school students, but is sometimes used by entering college students. For example, one student expressed a belief in the ability of science to solve problems as follows: "If scientific studies say [chemical additives in foods] cause cancer, then yes, they cause cancer. . . . If scientists prove they do [cause cancer] and if they put it on TV on the national news, then they have to be right."

Quasi-Reflective Thinking. By contrast, the reasoning typical of the middle stages (stages 4 and 5) is quasi-reflective. It is characterized by a recognition of the uncertainty of knowing (see Figures 2.4 and 2.5); thus, the thinker understands that some situations are truly problematic and that solutions for ill-structured problems are not absolutely certain. For individuals holding stage 4 and 5 assumptions, the difficulty lies in knowing how to make judgments in light of this uncertainty. These individuals typically argue that judgments ought to be based on evidence, but their evaluations are individualistic and idiosyncratic. Their acknowledgment that there are differences between well- and ill-structured problems is a developmental advance over the earlier stages; however, these individuals are often at a loss when asked to solve ill-structured

Figure 2.1. Pre-Reflective Thinking: Stage 1

"I know what I have seen."

View of Knowledge

Knowledge is assumed to exist absolutely and concretely; it is not understood as an abstraction. It can be obtained with certainty by direct observation.

Concept of Justification

Beliefs need no justification since there is assumed to be an absolute correspondence between what is believed to be true and what is true. Alternative beliefs are not perceived.

Source: Adapted from King and Kitchener, 1994.

Figure 2.2. Pre-Reflective Thinking: Stage 2

"If it is on the news, it has to be true."

View of Knowledge

Knowledge is assumed to be absolutely certain, or certain but not immediately available. Knowledge can be obtained directly through the senses (by direct observation) or from authority figures.

Concept of Justification

Beliefs are unexamined and unjustified, or are justified by their correspondence to the beliefs of an authority figure (such as a teacher or parent). Most issues are assumed to have a right answer, so there is little or no conflict in making decisions about disputed issues.

Source: Adapted from King and Kitchener, 1994.

Figure 2.3. Pre-Reflective Thinking: Stage 3

"When there is evidence that people can give to convince everybody one way or another, then it will be knowledge; until then, it's just a guess."

View of Knowledge

Knowledge is assumed to be absolutely certain or only temporarily uncertain. In areas of temporary uncertainty, only personal beliefs can be known until absolute knowledge is obtained. In areas of absolute certainty, knowledge is obtained from authorities.

Concept of Justification

In areas in which certain answers exist, beliefs are justified by reference to authorities' views. In areas in which answers do not exist, beliefs are defended as personal opinion since the link between evidence and beliefs is unclear.

Source: Adapted from King and Kitchener, 1994.

Figure 2.4. Quasi-Reflective Thinking: Stage 4

"I'd be more inclined to believe evolution if they had proof. It's just like the pyramids; I don't think we'll ever know. Who are you going to ask? No one was there."

View of Knowledge

Knowledge is uncertain and claims of knowledge are idiosyncratic, since situational variables (such as incorrect reporting of data, data lost over time, or disparities in access to data) dictate that knowing always involves an element of ambiguity.

Concept of Justification

Beliefs are justified by giving reasons and using evidence, but the arguments and choice of evidence are idiosyncratic—for example, evidence is chosen that fits an established belief.

Source: Adapted from King and Kitchener, 1994.

Figure 2.5. Quasi-Reflective Thinking: Stage 5

"People think differently and so they attack the problem differently. Other theories could be as true as my own, but based on different evidence."

View of Knowledge

Knowledge is contextual and subjective since it is filtered through individual perceptions and criteria for judgment. Only interpretations of evidence, events, or issues may be known.

Concept of Justification

Beliefs are justified within a particular context by using the rules of inquiry for that context and by context-specific interpretations of evidence. Specific beliefs are assumed to be context specific or are balanced against other interpretations, complicating (and sometimes delaying) conclusions.

Source: Adapted from King and Kitchener, 1994.

problems because they do not know how to deal with the problems' inherent ambiguity. For example, when asked whether a point of view about one ill-structured problem was right or wrong, one student responded: "I could not say one is right. That is why I said for you to get your information and I will get mine and we will compare it and see what comes out." We often find that college students hold assumptions like these and are perplexed about how to form a judgment when faced with uncertainty.

Reflective Thinking. Only when we interviewed advanced doctoral students and faculty members did we find individuals who were able both to acknowledge the uncertainty involved in ill-structured problem solving and to understand how evidence and interpretation of evidence could be defended as better, more credible, or best. It is reflective thinking like this that characterizes stages 6 and 7. The reasoning in these stages reveals the assumption that one's understanding of reality is not given but must be actively constructed and that knowledge must be understood in relationship to the context in which it was generated (see Figures 2.6 and 2.7). Further, individuals at these stages argue that some interpretations or knowledge claims may be judged as more plausible than others. Thus, even though absolute truth may never be achieved, these individuals suggest that some views may be evaluated as more or less truthful or reasonable explanations. This view presumes that judgments must be grounded in relevant data and must also be evaluated to determine their truth value. Criteria that might be used in such evaluations include conceptual soundness, coherence, and degree of fit with the data. In making judgments in this way, individuals are modeling truly reflective thinking. For example, when asked how she made a determination about what to believe in light of uncertainty, one person responded, "[I base my opinion on] how well thought out the positions are, at what level one chooses to argue the position, what kinds of reasoning and evidence one would use to support it, how it fits into the rest of one's worldview or rational explanation, how consistent the way in which one argues on this topic is as compared with other topics."

No single model of development can adequately describe all the complexities of human growth (let alone capture the mystery of it all). By the same token, no single model of intellectual development can capture and adequately describe all the complexities of human reasoning. Models can, however, provide heuristic tools educators may use to understand some basic differences in the ways students reason and make judgments. Models also can help faculty learn how to take these differences into account when encouraging students to think more reflectively and make more reasoned judgments. We offer the Reflective Judgment Model here as one such heuristic tool.

Figure 2.6. Reflective Thinking: Stage 6

"It's very difficult in this life to be sure. There are degrees of sureness. You come to a point at which you are sure enough for a personal stance on the issue."

View of Knowledge	Concept of Justification
Knowledge is constructed into individual conclusions about ill-structured problems based on information from a variety of sources. Interpretations that are based on evaluations of evidence across contexts and on the evaluated opinions of reputable others can be known.	Beliefs are justified by comparing evidence and opinion from different perspectives on an issue or across different contexts, and by constructing solutions that are evaluated by criteria such as the weight of the evidence, the utility of the solution, or the pragmatic need for action.

Source: Adapted from King and Kitchener, 1994.

Figure 2.7. Reflective Thinking: Stage 7

"One can judge arguments by how well thought out the positions are, what kinds of reasoning and evidence are used to support them, and how consistent the way one argues on this topic is as compared with other topics."

View of Knowledge	Concept of Justification
Knowledge is the outcome of a process of reasonable inquiry in which solutions to ill-structured problems are constructed. The adequacy of those solutions is evaluated in terms of what is most reasonable or probable based on the current evidence, and is reevaluated when relevant new evidence, perspectives, or tools of inquiry become available.	Beliefs are justified probabilistically, based on a variety of interpretive considerations such as the weight of the evidence, the explanatory value of the interpretations, the risk of erroneous conclusions, consequences of alternative judgments, and the interrelationships of these considerations. Conclusions are defended as representing the most complete, plausible, or compelling understanding of an issue, based on the available evidence.

Source: Adapted from King and Kitchener, 1994.

Research on the Reflective Judgment Model

Do college students reason reflectively about ill-structured problems? Does their reasoning improve with additional exposure to and involvement in higher education? To answer these questions, we present some of the major research findings on the Reflective Judgment Model. Many cross-sectional and longitudinal studies of college students have been conducted using the Reflective Judgment Interview (RJI) to investigate student reasoning about ill-structured problems. To date, more than 1,700 individuals representing a wide variety of student subgroups have been interviewed using the RJI. This number includes about 150 high school students, more than 1,100 college students (both traditional-age and adult samples), and about 200 graduate students. About 150 nonstudent adults have also been tested. The patterns of RJI scores from these studies (summarized in King and Kitchener, 1994) can inform educators' understanding of the development of students' reflective thinking in the context of higher education.

Figure 2.8 provides an overview of differences in reflective judgment by educational level from grade 9 through advanced doctoral study, based on a total sample of 1,334 traditional-aged students. As the figure illustrates, RJI scores increase by educational level, from high school to college and from college to graduate school. The middle line is the mean score for each educational level across all available samples; the top and bottom lines show the standard

Figure 2.8. Reflective Judgment Interview Scores, by Educational Level

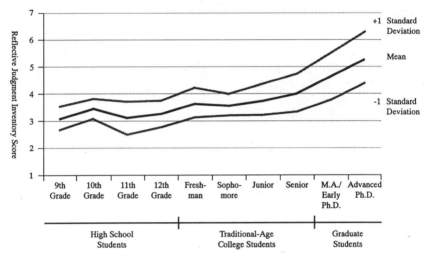

Note: Scores are averaged across all studies that reported RJI scores for students (N = 1,334) at these educational levels.

Source: King and Kitchener, 1994.

deviations across all these samples. The mean scores correspond to the stages of the Reflective Judgment Model: an RJI mean score of 3.0 for a given educational level indicates that the average stage usage for that educational level was stage 3.

The average RJI score for first-year college students is just above 3.5 (3.63). This means that these students' assumptions are most consistent with stages 3 and 4 of the Reflective Judgment Model and that at least some of the freshmen tested believed that absolute truth is only temporarily uncertain, that knowing is limited to personal beliefs about an issue (uninformed by evidence), and that most if not all problems are assumed to be well-structured. These students tend to have considerable difficulty in knowing what to believe or how to decide in the face of uncertainty. Frequently, they have difficulty relating evidence to their opinions, and fall back on simply believing what they want to believe at least until the truth is known. However, this figure also shows that about two-thirds of the freshmen tested are moving beyond stage 3 assumptions and are beginning to articulate the idea that uncertainty is an inherent characteristic of the process of knowing.

The highest average mean score for the college student samples was found for the seniors, 4.02. In contrast to the freshman samples, all the senior samples had an RJI mean score over 3.5, and half were over 4.0, a difference of about half a stage. This may not sound like an earthshaking difference, but while the numerical difference is small, it represents an important development in reasoning. The stage 4 reasoning that is prevalent among the senior samples is more adequate for solving ill-structured problems and more defensible by argument than the reasoning of less advanced students. As noted earlier, at stage 4, uncertainty is acknowledged as a persistent condition of knowing. It is also at this stage that students begin to use evidence systematically to support their judgments. As Barry Kroll (1992b) describes this type of development, students are abandoning "ignorant certainty" in favor of "intelligent confusion." Nevertheless, the seniors' mean score also suggests that many seniors are still confused when asked to defend their answers to ill-structured problems, arguing that a solution for such a problem is merely an opinion that cannot be defended as better than any other opinion. Since a major assumption of stage 4 is that there are many possible answers to every question and no absolutely certain way to adjudicate between competing answers, people who hold this assumption argue that knowledge claims are idiosyncratic. So while educators can take solace in the observation that students' movement toward being able to make reflective judgments is identifiable across educational levels, college seniors as a group show little evidence of being able to think reflectively, at least as we have defined it.

Because the data on which Figure 2.8 is based are cross-sectional, and because the means for the various educational levels are drawn from samples of varying size, we cannot determine whether the observed differences are due to the effects of aging, education, the interaction of aging and education, or whether they reflect cohort differences. The data do show, however, how traditional-age students typically score when asked to solve ill-structured problems.

Several groups of nontraditional-age freshmen and seniors have also been tested. The mean scores of these two classes (3.6 and 4.0, respectively) are identical to the mean scores for traditional-age freshmen and seniors (see King and Kitchener, 1994, for a full review of these data). On average, the ability of nontraditional-age undergraduates to understand the uncertainty of knowing and the use of evidence to generate a judgment about a complex problem is remarkably similar to the traditional-age undergraduate. In other words, age alone does not predict the ability to think reflectively.

While most of the students tested in the cross-sectional samples have been white, one study focused specifically on the educational experiences of African American students. Their Reflective Judgment scores were quite comparable to the mean scores of other freshmen, sophomores, and juniors, although the scores of the seniors were slightly lower. Obviously, more work is needed to evaluate whether there are important ethnic differences in how students construe knowledge and develop the ability to make reasoned judgments.

Gender differences have also been systematically studied in Reflective Judgment research. In seven of the fourteen studies that report gender differences (King and Kitchener, 1994), no gender differences were found. In the seven remaining studies, either men scored higher or there was a gender-by-class interaction. In a very provocative secondary analysis of gender issues, Wood (1993) found systematic differences in the timing of developmental growth spurts between men and women: women showed dramatic growth during their late teens and moderate increases later; men showed more evidence for growth during the mid-college and graduate student years. However, caution should be used in interpreting the RJI gender differences because the studies' sample selection criteria differed, and some studies did not control for the effects of academic ability (a consistent correlate of Reflective Judgment scores). Therefore, it is unclear whether the differences by gender that have been found result from differences in students' academic abilities, rates of maturation, times when growth in reflective judgment occurs, or opportunities to become involved in intellectually stimulating environments.

As noted earlier, the data discussed up to this point have been cross-sectional; thus, the differences in scores between educational levels could derive from a variety of sources and might not reflect real change. However, seven samples have been followed longitudinally for one to ten years. For virtually all of the traditional-age college student samples among these seven, there were consistent and significant increases in scores for all groups, even when the effects of verbal ability were controlled (King and Kitchener, 1994). In many cases, the longitudinal gains during the college years were much greater than is apparent in the cross-sectional data presented in Figure 2.8. Thus, based on the data collected to date, we believe that participation in higher education assists students to make more reflective judgments. Two sources of data inform our conclusion. In one longitudinal study, a group of high school students was followed and retested periodically for ten years (King and Kitchener, 1994). By the six-year testing (Kitchener, King, Wood, and Davison, 1989), the majority of the students had enrolled in college, and some had completed a bachelor's degree. All the students had been matched to a graduate sample on the basis of scholastic aptitude; thus, they had evidenced ability to complete at least a bachelor's degree. Despite the high scholastic ability of the whole sample, those who had completed a bachelor's degree had increased their RJI scores by one stage more than had those who did not graduate (a statistically significant difference). In other words, those who completed a college education showed more increase in their ability to reason reflectively than those who did not.

An additional study (Kitchener, Lynch, Fischer, and Wood, 1993) sheds further light on this issue. The purpose of this study was to investigate whether students would score higher in reflective judgment if they had the opportunity to practice and were provided with examples of higher-level reflective judgment responses. The answer to both questions was yes. Students scored at what we called their functional level when asked to respond in a typical interview setting to well-structured problems. However, when given cues about good responses and an opportunity to practice good responses, they scored substantially higher. We called this higher level their optimal level, since it seemed to represent the highest level the students could exhibit after practice and after having examined higher-stage responses. Nevertheless, even in such a supportive testing situation, most undergraduates—even seniors—were unable to understand a stage 7 statement well enough to explain it. This study suggests that with practice in making reflective judgments, students may be able to perform higher than either our cross-sectional or longitudinal data would suggest. It also suggests, however, that there may be an age-related ceiling on their competence, and that, even with practice, undergraduate students may not be able to score at the highest Reflective Judgment stages.

What is the role of education in the development of reflective thinking? Even though the data are not easily interpretable, and even though there are always variables that have not been (or cannot be) controlled and that may account for the obtained differences, nevertheless, it does appear that educational experiences can and do make a difference in whether or not individuals operate near their optimal level of reflective judgment. While a variety of experiences can potentially improve students' reflective thinking, education appears to play a stronger role in that improvement than do those experiences.

Educational Goals Reconsidered

The research described here adds force to the educational proposals recently offered by the Association for American Colleges as the foundation for reforming majors. Consider the following assertion: "By attending to the knowledge claims of the major over time and by treating increasingly complex matters from multiple points of view, students discover that nothing is self-evident, that nothing is simply 'there,' that questions and answers are chosen and created—not given—and that they always are framed by context; for that reason, they always are contingent" (Association of American Colleges, 1991, p. 13). The assumptions inherent in this statement, that knowledge is contextual and answers are contingent, are clearly consistent with stage 5 of the Reflective Judgment Model. Yet that is a full stage above where most college seniors tested to date have scored when tested using the RJI, and two stages below where faculty assume college seniors score (Dings, 1989). Nevertheless, this is still an appropriate goal! But students are not going to reach this goal if they are allowed to assume, for example, that facts are context free. Consider a second proposal: "Students cannot be allowed to be content with the notion that issues may be addressed by any number of equally valid formulations among which they cannot choose. They must learn to discriminate by arguing, and they must realize that arguments exist for the purpose of clarifying and making choices" (Association of American Colleges, 1991, p. 14). Students at all educational levels make choices and judgments, but at the earlier levels, their judgments are based on unexamined convictions rather than a process of deliberation and critical inquiry. The student skills the AAC proposal seeks are associated with learning to discriminate the valid from the invalid (or less valid) formulations and are found in stages 6 and 7 of the Reflective Judgment Model, along with the ability to make discriminating arguments. Faculty who attempt to teach this reasoning process may need to provide many opportunities for students to practice and refine the skills associated with it and should not assume that students arrive at college able to make and defend such reflective judgments. As noted earlier, however, because there is a difference between students' functional levels of reasoning and their optimal levels, reached after they have been given the opportunity to model and practice higher-level reasoning, they may be able to use reasoning a stage or two higher than is typical for the majority of undergraduates.

Suggestions for Teaching Reflective Thinking

Despite the value educators place on students' use of the reasoning skills associated with the higher stages of Reflective Judgment, it is important that educators accept and respect students at whatever judgment levels they exhibit. While the characteristics of the early stages of Reflective Judgment are not consistent with true reflective thinking, they do reveal the genuine assumptions about knowledge and how it is gained that some students use to solve controversial problems. These assumptions can be the building blocks for higher stages of understanding and resolving problems. They are also a window through which faculty can observe the beliefs students typically use when solving ill-structured problems. Therefore, it is important for teachers to accept and support students when challenging student reasoning, and to understand that a strong internal logic exists in the patterns of reasoning at each stage (including the early stages, which often appear illogical to educators). The teacher's understanding may make the student more receptive when the teacher points out the insufficiencies of the early stages. It may also make students more willing to take the intellectual risks associated with abandoning old, comfortable ways of thinking.

Thinking, reasoning, and judging are the heart of the intellectual process. Encouraging students to develop the habits of mind associated with reflective thinking and teaching them the importance of these skills are among a college's most important responsibilities. Moreover, as educators address this responsibility, they should remember that many factors influence the process of learning to make reflective judgments: the student's established reasoning skills, his or her emotional readiness to defend a point of view, the educational values emphasized in the student's college, the teacher's favorite strategies and assumptions about how students learn, and the broader societal norms and expectations for reasoned discourse about current events. Learning to think reflectively occurs within the context of an intellectual community, and this community ranges from the immediate environment of a student's living group or specific class to the broader college community and its environs.

Each community has special opportunities for and limitations to teaching students to think reflectively. If a community is intellectually alive, vibrant, and eager to do what it takes to support and challenge students to think reflectively, then the intellectual impact of that community can be powerful and enduring.

As suggested by The Challenge of Connecting Learning, "the role of faculty members is to provide structures and languages . . . that enhance and challenge students' capacities to frame issues, to test hypotheses and arguments against evidence, and to address disputed claims" (Association of American Colleges, 1991, pp. 4–5). What kinds of teaching strategies and learning environments do instructors use and create in order to fulfill this role? Deciding what to teach requires not only a thorough knowledge of a discipline, but a vision of the kind of person the college or university, as an educating community, seeks to develop. This vision should include the designation of common abilities as goals for the early, middle, and later parts of study in a major. Reflective thinking is a fundamental ability that connects learning across many majors. The issues of how individuals can know, what they can know, and how they can approach ill-structured problem solving are not the domain of the study of English or rhetoric or philosophy or any other discipline; they are common to the humanities and the social sciences as well as the sciences. Problems across many disciplines require reflective thinking.

We do not want to leave the impression, however, that a curriculum focused on inquiry about discipline-specific ill-structured problems is devoid of content. A curriculum that is deliberately structured to promote inquiry about ill-structured problems can give students facing the hard problems of the adult world an important model of how to think about such problems, but only if that curriculum imparts an accurate understanding of the necessary knowledge base (carbon and hydrogen do not combine to form oak!).

What, then, does the Reflective Judgment Model suggest the curriculum should include? First, it suggests that ill-structured, contestable problems within each discipline need to be identified and shared with students. They should not be secrets that scholars keep to themselves until students reach graduate school. Students engage in reflective thinking only while they are considering ill-structured problems; thus, familiarizing students with such problems not only gives them a diverse set of opportunities for practicing reflective reasoning skills, it legitimizes the process of questioning what is known and helps students learn better ways of addressing such problems. We recognize, however, that this sharing of problems may be easier said than done. Consider the following report from an instructor of environmental science: "Major conceptual ideas in ecology are still debated regularly, with no end to the debate in sight. So I try to present both sides, even in introductory ecology. However, no matter how hard I try, this baffles the students. I recently got a memorable comment on a teacher evaluation form: 'Don't tell us what the controversies are. Tell us LIKE IT IS!!'" (M. Palmer, personal communication to Patricia King, September 23, 1992).

Second, the Reflective Judgment Model suggests that, early in their college years, many students will be struggling with issues of certainty and uncertainty. Therefore, even introductory courses should be structured to provide students with opportunities to consider opposing views on the controversial issues within the discipline.

Third, the model suggests that faculty should create occasions for students in their later college years to practice constructing judgments in light of uncertainty, to learn how to think about the relationship between evidence and a point of view, to learn how to evaluate evidence on different sides of an issues, and to analyze the role and presumed importance of objectivity. While undergraduate students may not become reflective thinkers in the most complex and advanced sense, we believe they can come much closer to that goal than they currently do. Think of what educators might accomplish if they structured their teaching and the curriculum to promote reflective thinking!

In addition, understanding that students differ by virtue of their conceptual orientations toward knowledge and the justification of beliefs allows educators to respond to those differences on an individual basis. For example, Kroll (1992a) suggests the following strategies: "When [students'] responses are dogmatic, I foster all their doubts; when they seem mired in skepticism or paralyzed by complexity, I push them to make judgments; when their tactics are not fully reflective, I encourage their best efforts to use critical, interrogative, or evaluative thinking" (p. 13). In other words, instructors should encourage reflective thinking where they see it and foster students' willingness to decide on the basis of inquiry. Other examples of ways instructors have structured courses to promote reflective thinking may be found in the special issue of Liberal Education (1992) devoted to reflective judgment; King and Kitchener (1994); and Kitchener and King (1990).

As you think about how to promote reflective thinking in the major, we suggest that you consider the following questions.*

What are your own assumptions about knowledge and knowing? What are your field's assumptions about knowledge and knowing? How do you come to know what you claim to know in your field?

What are considered to be facts in your discipline? Are theories presented as the territory itself or as the map of the territory (a map that may have topographical effects)?

What are the methods of inquiry in your discipline? Do you strive for objectivity? If so, what does that mean? What intellectual values do the methods reflect?

Are courses sequenced in a manner that is consistent with increasing intellectual demands on students and helping them attain necessary skills?

How do you define critical thinking in your discipline? Is this definition (along with its associated skills) limited to well-structured problems?

* Some of these are based on ideas shared by Finster (1992).

With what degree of certainty can you "know something" in your discipline? What would you offer as examples?

Does our culture hold assumptions about science, history, and art that undermine our ability to use the knowledge and insights from these fields in societal decisions?

Do you discuss questions such as these directly with students? Do students have opportunities to learn how and why you answer these questions as you do?

In conclusion, what we have observed over the last fifteen years is that, between childhood and the young-adult years, people's assumptions about knowledge change in somewhat predictable ways and that changes in these assumptions lead to corresponding changes in how students understand and justify their beliefs when they are faced with ill-structured problems. Further, we have found that participation in higher education seems to be associated with the attainment of the skills associated with the higher stages of Reflective Judgment. The educational activities that are associated with the attainment of reflective thinking skills involve students' being challenged to wrestle with ill-structured problems and receiving cognitive and emotional support to do so. Faculty need to focus as much on teaching students how to question assumptions and raise questions as on teaching students how to arrive at solutions to questions.

We close this chapter with the words of a student who, after graduating from college, shared some encouraging thoughts with the instructor of a freshman writing course designed to promote reflective thinking. (The course is discussed in Kroll, 1992a, b.) The course had been structured around the theme of the Vietnam War, and the student wrote: "Hope you're still teaching the Vietnam class. I feel it was one of the most important courses I had. And not just because it dealt with the Vietnam War. Rather, your course taught something all college courses should, but for the most part don't strive for: how to think. By coping, discussing, and trying to come to terms with many difficult, thought-provoking, and largely unanswerable issues, I learned more in your class than I did in many other classes combined" (1992b, p. 13). Such responses strengthen our conviction that courses that focus on inquiry can promote reflective thinking.

References

Association of American Colleges. Liberal Learning and the Arts and Sciences Major. Vol. 1: The Challenge of Connecting Learning. Washington, D.C.: Association of American Colleges, 1991.

Barry, D. Toledo Magazine. November 1, 1981.

Bowen, H. R. Investment in Learning: The Individual and Social Value of American Higher Education. San Francisco: Jossey-Bass, 1977.

Churchman, C. W. The Design of Inquiring Systems: Basic Concepts of Systems and Organizations. New York: Basic Books, 1971.

Dewey, J. How We Think: A Restatement of the Relation of Reflective Thinking to the Educative Process. Lexington, Mass.: Heath, 1933.

Dings, J. G. "Faculty Members' Assumptions About College Students' Cognitive Development." Unpublished master's thesis, Department of College Student Personnel, Bowling Green State University, 1989.

Facione, P. A. "Critical Thinking: A Statement of Expert Consensus for Purposes of Educational Assessment and Instruction." Research findings and recommendations prepared for the Committee on Pre-College Philosophy of the American Philosophical Association, 1990.

Finster, D. C. "New Pathways for Teaching Chemistry: Reflective Judgment in Science." Liberal Education, 1992, 78 (1), 14–19.

King, P. M., and Kitchener, K. S. Developing Reflective Judgment: Understanding and Promoting Intellectual Growth and Critical Thinking in Adolescents and Adults. San Francisco: Jossey-Bass, 1994.

Kitchener, K. S., and King, P. M. "Reflective Judgment: Concepts of Justification and Their Relationship to Age and Education." Journal of Applied Developmental Psychology, 1981, 2, 89–116.

Kitchener, K. S., and King, P. M. "The Reflective Judgment Model: Transforming Assumptions About Knowing." In J. Mezirow and Associates, Fostering Critical Reflection in Adulthood: A Guide to Transformative and Emancipatory Learning. San Francisco: Jossey-Bass, 1990.

Kitchener, K. S., King, P. M., Wood, P. K., and Davison, M. L. "Consistency and Sequentiality in the Development of Reflective Judgment: A Six Year Longitudinal Study." Journal of Applied Developmental Psychology, 1989, 10, 73–95.

Kitchener, K. S., Lynch, C., Fischer, K. W., and Wood, P. K. "Development Range of Reflective Judgment: The Effect of Contextual Support and Practice on Developmental Stage." Journal of Applied Developmental Psychology, 1993, 29 (5), 893–906.

Kroll, B. M. "Reflective Inquiry in a College English Class." Liberal Education, 1992a, 78 (1), 10–13.

Kroll, B. M. Teaching Hearts and Minds: College Students Reflect on the Vietnam War in Literature. Carbondale: Southern Illinois University Press, 1992b.

Kurfiss, J. G. "Critical Thinking: Theory, Research, Practice and Possibilities." ASHE-ERIC Higher Education Report No. 2. Washington, D.C.: Association for the Study of Higher Education, 1988.

Liberal Education, Jan.–Feb. 1992 (entire issue).

Pascarella, E. T., and Terenzini, P. T. How College Affects Students: Findings and Insights from Twenty Years of Research. San Francisco: Jossey-Bass, 1991.

Weingartner, R. Undergraduate Education. New York: Macmillan, 1991.

Wood, P. K. "Context and Development of Reflective Thinking: A Secondary Analysis of the Structure of Individual Differences." Unpublished paper, 1993.

PATRICIA M. KING is associate professor and acting chair, Department of Higher Education and Student Affairs, Bowling Green State University.

KAREN STROHM KITCHENER is professor and director, Counseling Psychology Division, College of Education, University of Denver.

Liberal education is commonly valued for fostering general intel-
lectual development while challenging parochialism, yet recent
studies show that students must internalize the mental worlds of
particular communities to engage in persuasive analysis and argu-
ment. In what sense, then, can a major provide liberal learning?

Enculturation or Critical Engagement?

Carol Geary Schneider

> At its best, liberal learning extends beyond particular subject mat-
> ter, which inevitably changes over time, to instill qualities of mind.
> —Association of American Colleges (1989)

The discipline and furniture of the mind, mental powers, analytical capacities, reflective judgment—these descriptive phrases have evolved over two centuries of conversation about the purposes and effects of U.S. higher education. Whatever the language used in their rhetoric, faculty have constantly maintained a focus on students' development of usable mental capacities, both as a justification for the importance of higher learning and as an expectation about its lasting effects. As Ernest Pascarella and Patrick Terenzini (1991) observe in their recent synthesis of twenty years of research on the effects of college:

> Abundant evidence suggests that much factual material is forgotten rather soon after it is presented in educational settings. . . . Thus, beyond postsecondary education's undeniably significant role in the imparting of specific subject matter knowledge, claims for the enduring influence of postsecondary education on learning must be based, to some extent at least, on the fostering of a repertoire of general intellectual or cognitive competencies and skills. These cognitive skills go by a number of different names (reasoning skills, critical thinking, intellectual flexibility, reflective judgment, cognitive complexity, and so on), and they differ somewhat in the types of problems or issues they address. . . . These cognitive competencies and skills represent the general intellectual outcomes of college. . . .

[They] are a particularly important resource for the individual in a society and world where factual knowledge is becoming obsolete at an accelerated rate [1991, pp. 114–115].

As we would hope, the research evidence reviewed in Pascarella and Terenzini's important book provides substantial if uneven evidence that college positively affects students' cognitive abilities. Students make "statistically significant gains during the college years on a number of dimensions of general cognitive capabilities and skills," and at least part of these gains can be attributed specifically to college attendance rather than general maturation (Pascarella and Terenzini, 1991, p. 155). Moreover, students' particular choices of majors are not significantly linked to their gains on measures of critical abilities although, unsurprisingly, students do better when a measure of critical ability is similar in structure to problems encountered in their particular major.

Yet a close analysis of some of these reported findings on student learning in college suggests a less positive view than Pascarella and Terenzini report, a view similar in substance to many faculty members' own increasingly unflattering private descriptions of college students' reasoning and communication abilities. Examining reasoning both in the academy and beyond, a number of cognitive researchers argue what common sense would also suggest: that adult life requires the cognitive capacities to make sense of multiplicity, to sort among competing claims and assertions, to consider positions in light of both evidence and values, and to construct a grounded analysis that takes into account the varieties of evidence and the strength of opposing positions. In simpler words, in a world where difference is a given and certainty in short supply, adults must develop their own analyses, make their own arguments.

In this context, King and Kitchener's one and one-half decades of findings on students' development of reflective judgment during the college years, usefully summarized in Chapter Two, should give us pause. Though Pascarella and Terenzini cite King and Kitchener's research as evidence of the positive effects of college on cognitive skills, King and Kitchener themselves note that faculty members' normative standards for reasoning in college reveal that faculty expect a level of both skill and intellectual self-awareness well beyond what most students apparently achieve. As King and Kitchener point out, *The Challenge of Connecting Learning,* the Association of American Colleges (AAC) study of the major, argues that students should learn "to state why a question or argument is significant and for whom; what the difference is between developing and justifying a position and merely asserting one; and how to develop and provide warrants for their own interpretations and judgments" (Association of American Colleges, 1991, p. 14). Yet, King and Kitchener (Chapter Two) report, "many seniors are still confused when asked to defend their answers to ill-structured problems, arguing that a solution for such a problem is merely an opinion that cannot be defended as better than any other. . . . As a group, [college seniors] show little evidence of being able to think reflectively, at least as we have defined it." King and Kitchener also report that faculty members assume students reason at higher stages of the reflective judgment model than they actually do.

If multiplicity is what characterizes the modern world, many college graduates appear inadequately prepared to bring reflective, grounded judgments to bear on that multiplicity. Not recognizing their teachers' working assumption that different domains have their own standards for judgment and evidence, students encounter diversity and label it babel, opinion, or academic games. The acerbic comments from faculty at one public college, for example, illuminate the distance between what standardized tests may report and college faculties' own working standards of judgment. Using a nationally normed test of general college outcomes, this college found that on several measures (for example, communication and research, critical thinking, values clarification, and the like) the college's students both made gains across their four years of study and exceeded national norms. Yet the college's faculty members, when presented with these findings, were unconvinced and unimpressed. Instead they asked, "If this writing is at the 60th percentile, what must it be like to teach in the rest of the country?" (Curry and Hager, 1987, p. 62).

Mental Discipline and the Liberal Arts Major

Whatever foundation for acquiring analytical and communication capabilities may be laid in general education courses, students' developed abilities in these areas must be seen as an integral and central responsibility of liberal arts majors. Majors in arts and sciences disciplines emerged as a standard feature of liberal education in the reflected glow of new enthusiasm about disciplinary potential to uncover the essential secrets of nature and human society. Arts and sciences subjects made their initial case for a central place in the college curriculum in the first decades of the twentieth century not simply as a way of bringing order to the confusions of the then-reigning elective system but also because they were expected to help students develop mental discipline. Claims once advanced to defend the study of Greek and Latin as an essential core curriculum that would train mental capacities were successively appropriated by new arts and sciences fields as they contended for legitimacy within the standard curriculum. Each of the emerging disciplinary fields, from chemistry to literature, aspired to some version of systematic or scientific inquiry. The study of literature, for example, entered the research academy as philology, thus making the same claims to become a science advanced by physics, biology, and chemistry. Students' immersion in the methods as well as the findings of a particular scholarly discipline, adherents claimed, would help students develop both methods of inquiry and systematic knowledge. Thus, even as specialized arts and sciences majors displaced the common curricula of the nineteenth-century college, each major also assumed separate responsibility for what early nineteenth-century scholars had described as a college's fundamental commitment to "call into daily and vigorous effort the faculties of the student" (cited in Rudolph, 1977, p. 68).

It is educational commitment to foster critical inquiry, analysis, and reflective judgment that is still thought to distinguish study in a liberal arts field from study in a preprofessional subject. Preprofessional studies, so conventional academic wisdom insists, impart technique and know-how rather than insight and judgment. The result is that "in many fields, skills have become ends. . . . We are turning out technicians. But the crisis of our time relates not to technical competence, but to a loss of social and historical perspective, to the disastrous divorce of competence from conscience. . . . Professionals . . . must respond to questions [about] 'why'" (Boyer, 1987, pp. 110–111). Liberal arts fields, by contrast, are supposed to teach students how to question assumptions and push beyond the limits of the given. Hence the conventional equation of liberal arts fields with a cosmopolitan perspective. Assumed to teach students a critical stance and ways of discovering knowledge for themselves, arts and sciences majors are usually defended as forms of study that free students from parochial perspectives and prepare them to deal with complexity, contingency, and the certainty of change.

Disciplinary Enculturation

In recent years, a number of cautionary notes have emerged about this positive picture of the liberating learning and intellectual development supposedly found in liberal arts fields. In 1985, the Association of American Colleges (AAC) sounded a challenge to the traditional justifications of what it called study in depth when it released Integrity in the College Curriculum. In that report, a distinguished group of scholar–teachers and academic administrators had harsh words for the major:

> The undergraduate major . . . everywhere dominates, but the nature and degree of that concentration varies widely and irrationally from college to college. Indeed, the major in most colleges is little more than a gathering of courses taken in one department, lacking structure and depth, as is often the case in the humanities and social sciences, or emphasizing content to the neglect of the essential style of inquiry on which the content is based, as is too frequently true in the natural and physical sciences. The absence of a rationale for the major becomes transparent . . . where the essential message embedded in all the [catalogue] prose is: pick eight of the following [Association of American Colleges, 1985, p. 2].

Integrity called particular attention to the political settlements behind the departmental curriculum. Far from offering students systematic and developmental apprenticeships in using the approaches of a field, the AAC panel argued, many majors have allowed "coverage" to take the place of giving students practice in using the disciplines (pp. 27–28). Faculty appointments at the departmental level are made to reflect the major subfields within a discipline; curricular requirements mirror and support this academic division of labor. In place of educational purpose and plan, the liberal arts major too often offers students a cafeteria menu of courses designed to acknowledge the faculty's scholarly interests rather than to provide a coherent and developmental program of study. Such major requirements ensure coverage of disciplinary subfields; their capacity to guide analytical practice and the development of competence in using disciplinary methods is far less certain.

AAC's stringent critique of the state of study in depth might well be construed as no more than a call to honor a long-standing equation of disciplinary method with critical thinking and thereby to restructure majors along principles of guided disciplinary practice as well as content coverage. Study in depth, said Integrity, should provide "a central core of method and theory that serves as an introduction to the explanatory power of the discipline" and provides a framework for subsequent learning (Association of American Colleges, 1985, p. 29). Many of Integrity's readers understood this statement to mean that the liberal arts major should recommit itself to teach disciplinary methods of inquiry and analysis as well as particular knowledge.

But even as AAC seemed to call for studies in depth to redeem the founding claims for disciplinary fields as contexts for mental discipline and reflective judgment, research in fields as various as rhetoric, English composition, linguistics, and cognitive science, and epistemological studies across the disciplines, cast doubt on the founding claims themselves. From many quarters, new studies of disciplinary ethos and practice have raised fundamental questions about both the assumed scientific neutrality of disciplinary method and about the capacity of learning in a discipline to develop general cognitive skills and capabilities. As we will see in the remainder of this chapter, an important vein of scholarly analysis now views disciplines not as combinations of topics and potentially illuminating research methods but as discrete and highly enclosed discourse communities, cut off from one another as well as from nonacademic communities by the barriers of special languages and exclusionary cultural norms. Within these communities, knowledge construction is governed by internal rules, both tacit and explicit, about what is already known, what is assumed, what counts as evidence, and how analysis must be presented. This view calls into question the widespread assumption that college can—and should—teach general models for "good" reasoning and its close ally "good" writing. The standards for both vary with each discipline. What persuades in the psychology department will be received with skepticism in the economics department; arguments out of both these camps will be firmly charged with the crime of egregious writing by the English department.

Jonathan Smith's incisive comments on the disciplines and liberal learning (Chapter One) illustrate a fundamental strand in the emerging view that disciplinary learning involves intellectual enculturation rather than intellectual

liberation. In this view, the disciplines do not impart neutral scientific procedures for analysis and investigation. Much less do they teach a general set of
cognitive skills that enable discourse across disciplinary lines. What argument
within a disciplinary framework requires, growing numbers of scholars con-
tend, is enculturation, socialization into a particular way of looking at the
world, a particular set of assumptions that govern argument but that also,
because they are widely internalized within the field itself, are rarely opened
to searching scrutiny or debate. As Smith and a growing band of scholars suggest, ordinary discourse within a department and its parent field too often
excludes second-order reflection on the field itself. Even when a field is riven
with profound debates about disciplinary ethos and method—as many of the
social sciences and humanities currently are—the major is rarely organized to
help students engage those debates directly and consider either their significance or the grounds behind the competing claims. Small wonder, we may well
think, that students graduating from college are uncertain about the nature of
argument, the existence of standards for evidence, or the possibility of relating
findings to context, as King and Kitchener report (Chapter Two). For within
the interpretive communities we call disciplines, these matters are seldom open
to examination from multiple critical points of view, even though such matters
are central to the work of disciplines and to the claims of the academy to free
students from parochial frames of reference.

    By its general organization, a college or university exposes its students to
many disciplinary perspectives. What it does not provide are either methods
or venues for thinking about the relations among these perspectives: their com-
plementarity, their dissonance, the bases for their competing claims. In virtually all liberal arts fields, students learn that some points are self-evident; they
do not learn that self-evidence is itself a field-specific claim. Mediocre students
may spend their entire college careers uncertain how to judge or manage the
multiplicity that characterizes the academy; it is these students who show up
on developmental studies as multiplists or, in King and Kitchener's term
(Chapter Two), "quasi-reflective thinkers," cognizant that diversity marks all
intellectual discourse but firmly persuaded that there are no ways to choose
among competing claims. The arts and sciences students that faculty consider
successful acquire intellectual blinders as well because, to work effectively
within a disciplinary framework, these successful students must internalize a
set of field-specific assumptions and perspectives that may impede rather than
foster critical dialogue and engaged debate across disciplinary boundaries.

    English composition studies offer an especially acute analysis of discipli-
nary enculturation. In an arresting if sobering portrait, David Russell summa-
rizes the emerging view of what actually happens as students learn to make
arguments within a particular disciplinary context. If writing and rhetoric are
"deeply embedded in the differentiated practices of disciplines," then writing
is not "a single elementary skill," and learning to write is actually "a process of
socialization or acculturation. . . . The neophyte gradually acquires the com-

munity's shared knowledge not only by listening and reading but also by experimenting with verbal formulations, orally . . . and later in writing" (1991, p. 15). Russell stresses that learning to write by "this gradual and often-subtle process of observation, modeling, and intervention requires the neophyte to use the language of the community while participating in its activity not before participating." It is through such participation that a student comes to connect the verbal formulations he or she is learning to the community's meanings and to "learn not only the community's terms and categories but also when and how to apply them: the interactional rules. . . . Eventually, the neophyte so thoroughly internalizes the discourse of the community and, with it, the community's perceptions, assumptions, and behaviors, that she begins to think and act—and write—like a member of the community" (1991, pp. 16–18).

What Russell describes, of course, is the successful neophyte, the student who eventually masters, at least at an intermediate level, the rules of a community's written and verbal discourse. Russell's tale is echoed by research on students' own perceptions of learning to think in academic settings. Belenkey, Clinchy, Goldberger, and Tarule (1986), for example, studying women's experiences of learning in college, capture the voices of women very much aware of following others' prescribed methods for analysis and writing and caught unhappily between the perception that these methods are alien and the recognition that they are what the faculty want. The many students who do not learn the prescribed rules and methods either fall away or persist on the boundaries of the discipline, paining their instructors with the naive and awkward quality of their writing and argument. Yet this learning process, as Russell points out, is invisible to or "misinterpreted" by the students' instructors. They themselves have so internalized the strategies of the discipline they teach that they "often cannot see or understand why others, who are writing about the same 'content' do not 'make sense.' Though the students may understand the 'facts,' they may not understand the essential rhetorical structures: specialized lines of argument, vocabulary, and organizational conventions, the tacit understandings about what must be stated and what assumed—in short, the culture of the discipline that gives meaning to the 'facts'" (1991, p. 18).

Is the Liberal Arts Major Obsolete?

The emerging view of the enculturative requirements for thinking and writing in the disciplines raises an important challenge to liberal arts majors' traditional claims to foster critical reasoning and reflective judgment. Conventionally, these capacities are seen as transcultural rather than context-bound skills, opening doors beyond local prejudices and viewpoints, making and marking citizens of the world. The major—and especially the liberal arts major—is supposed to provide a passport to all parts of the globe, not incorporation into the student's choice among modern monasteries. In this research on disciplinary socialization, as in so many other intellectual arenas, postmodern scholarship is busily undoing the universalistic assumptions of the Enlightenment, the values that formed the modern university and still provide rationales for many of its espoused goals and educational procedures.

However, it may be that if we had not already invented departmental majors we would discover that something like them is needed in the modern academy. For even as scholarship on rhetoric and composition illuminates the enculturative dimensions of learning in a specific field, research on the development of higher-order reasoning makes a strong case that such enculturation is a necessary and integral dimension of intellectual development. What we find in a large body of research on reasoning and argumentation, usefully summarized by Perkins and Salomon (1989), is persuasive evidence that these highly valued intellectual capacities are, by nature, situated and contextual rather than general and decontextualized. Or, to put it differently, cognitive strategies are least powerful when very general, most effective when linked to context, to well-organized knowledge bases, and to communally negotiated standards for marshalling evidence, analysis, and argument.

Research on novice and expert reasoning forcefully illustrates the importance of well-structured knowledge bases in complex reasoning. When confronted with complex questions, novices address the surface features of the problem (Glaser, 1984). Knowing little of the context from which a particular problem emerges, or of earlier attempts to address the problem, they attempt to solve it at its most superficial level. If they know nothing about a topic, they may resort to conventional wisdom as a source of insight: for example, "We can't do anything about gridlock in Washington because all politicians are greedy." Possessed of a bit more information, they weave it into something superficially resembling an analysis: for example, "the structure of the constitution makes political gridlock inevitable." Experts, by contrast, draw on richly developed knowledge bases to explore the nuances of a problem; they spend much more time than novices developing complex representations of a problem—its dimensions, complexities, and potential ways of viewing and interpreting it. Thus, the expert weaves information into a complex analysis: for example, "One school of thought holds that the ending of the Cold War has fundamentally shifted the relationship between presidential leadership and the members of Congress, leading to greater likelihood that the Congress will reject presidential initiatives. On the other hand, we have seen similar assertions of congressional authority in other transitional periods, such as the period following the Civil War." In each of these examples, the quality of the knowledge base strongly affects the quality of the analysis. Lacking knowledge, the student has nothing out of which to construct an argument.

In a classic piece of research, James Voss and his colleagues at the University of Pittsburgh illustrated the relationship between knowledge and analytical ability in an experiment that challenged social scientists, chemists, and novices to address the problem of agriculture in what was then the Soviet Union (Voss, Greene, Post, and Penner, 1983). Participants were given a brief description of the issue, and Voss then recorded and analyzed the arguments each subject developed to address the problem. He found that the chemists' way of framing the problem was more like that of novices than that of the expert social scientists. Absent a knowledge base relevant to Soviet agricultural difficulties, the chemists' analytical capacities, sophisticated though they were in matters of chemistry, became novice-like in relation to the problem posed. The chemists could not develop complex arguments about the Soviet agricultural problem because they lacked the information to do so.

Sophisticated reasoning requires extensive procedural as well as content knowledge. Beyond information, experts also command well-structured and often routinized analytical structures for organizing, interpreting, and presenting information. Sometimes simply classifying a problem produces a well-established procedure for addressing it: "Oh, that's essentially a supply and demand problem," the economist will say, and present a quick and straightforward analysis. But, often, a problem is open ended, and the expert then has to make a case both as to what information counts and why that information matters. In either case, experts draw on well-developed procedural knowledge about how to make a persuasive argument. The historian of Congress knows, for example, that his fellow historians are not likely to be persuaded by a paper that explains political behavior in terms of the protagonists' childhood experiences. The effective political activist knows that her followers are not likely to be moved to action by a lengthy historical analysis of congressional problems. To be persuasive, and therefore effective, each must use a rhetorical and organizational strategy appropriate to the audience at hand. Here we come back to Russell's portrait of the novice learning to use the language of the community: the historian of Congress can persuade fellow historians—or at least compel a hearing—because he knows, from within, the assumptions, evidentiary standards, and rhetorical strategies used by historians. The effective political activist has learned how activists (and followers) think and learn; she persuades them as she makes an argument in a form they can understand and follow.

These findings on higher-order reasoning reaffirm the importance of work in a focused discourse or interpretive community that provides a context for students' intellectual development. Equally important, they highlight a dual agenda for those who teach in such interpretive communities. Effective study in depth should provide students with opportunities to develop well-structured and integrated knowledge about a designated set of issues, concepts, and topics; it should also provide guided practice in making increasingly complex arguments that use the concepts and analytical methods of the designated field. These two tasks cannot be left to chance, nor is either task alone a satisfactory orientation to the practice of critical inquiry. Students' acquisition of knowledge and of the ability to use that knowledge in making analyses and arguments are both important responsibilities of the liberal arts major.

From Enculturation to Critical Engagement

Does enculturation in a discipline encompass all that we mean by liberal learning? Surely not. The process I have described here teaches a student to work within a community, to speak a restricted language, and to explore the uses of that language and its grammar in framing and examining specific kinds of knowledge. But certainly, as Elaine Maimon suggests in Chapter Six, we want our students to be able to work in multiple communities, to speak more than one language. Given the complexity of the world around us, any individual is hindered if he or she can speak only one language, perform in only one context. Preparation for the modern world requires practice in translating languages, negotiating differences, rethinking one's understandings in light of alternative conceptual frames and points of view.

What this goal suggests is that the work of the major is only half done when students have learned to speak the language of one community well enough to use it in discussion and argument. To engage in critical dialogue, students must encounter more than one community, more than one means of making an argument. They must know something about, for example, how historians work and also how political activists engage colleagues, followers, and opponents. They cannot be expected to develop such knowledge by taking simply one course in history and another in parties and politics. Distributional requirements that lead students to take an array of requirements in different fields, ostensibly to expose the students to disparate ways of knowing, ignore the relational dimension of learning. The history major needs to explore the reasons why history carries less weight than might be hoped with activists; the political activist needs to counter her own analyses with the perspectives and analytical approaches of reflective disciplines. Both of them need to recognize that both history and commitment may have very different meanings in societies other than those they encounter in the United States.

What all of this suggests, then, is that majors, with their structured introduction to a particular field and worldview, are necessary but not sufficient to the kind of liberal learning that we espouse in the academy and require in the wider world. Liberal arts majors can and should provide apprenticeships in particular strategies for thinking, analysis, and argument, but these strategies must be complemented by deliberately countervailing perspectives, strategies, and experiences if students are to recognize the strengths, limitations, and best uses of the points of view they develop in their initial college studies. Genuine critical engagement always involves translation and negotiation as well as argument; students need experiences of taking their arguments and knowledge into disparate contexts and learning to deal with the challenges they will inevitably find there. These experiences of translation and negotiation should extend, moreover, beyond the academic realm. There is a cultural chasm between the world of structured knowledge and the world of practice. If we expect students to use wisely the knowledge and perspective they acquire in the academy, we ought to guide them through experiences in distilling the interrelationships between knowledge acquired through analysis and knowledge developed through practice. Nor is attention to learning out of school a distraction from the academy's central concerns. Resnick (1987) reports that programs designed to teach critical thinking are most successful when they incorporate the contextual and social features of learning in nonacademic settings.

What then of liberal learning in a disciplinary major? On the one hand, we see that learning in a major is an enculturative process that teaches prescribed and delimited ways of thinking. On the other hand, a well-established tradition of scholarship shows that specific ways of thinking, once acquired, do not readily transfer or generalize to other domains (Perkins and Salomon, 1989). Our successful student, properly socialized, has learned to think like an economist or a philosopher or an accountant. But thinking in particular frames of reference does not, by itself alone, provide students with the capabilities and perspectives they need to traverse the wider world's many knowledge communities and cultures.

Examining these complications in the work of a liberal arts major leads us to a complex view of the responsibilities of liberal learning. There is certainly a case to be made for the major's role in teaching a particular discipline as a foundational apprenticeship in inquiry and analysis. The question is not whether such learning is valuable, but whether, as Integrity argued, the typical organization of the major actually provides guided opportunities for analytical practice and growing sophistication. But there is equally a case to be made for the major's work as integrative and translational or intercultural learning. A student learning the approaches of one field ought to be expected to juxtapose those approaches with the perspectives, values, and contributions of other fields. Students who elect minors and/or double majors should be expected to connect and consider the relations between their disparate studies; students who do neither should be expected to develop minors and/or cognate studies related to their majors that introduce alternative disciplinary perspectives. All students ought to have experiences of learning in nonacademic settings and of reflecting with others on that learning.

When students extend their focused studies beyond departmental and/or disciplinary boundaries, they can begin to perceive both the power and the limits not just of a discipline but of communities themselves as makers and authorizers of knowledge. We cannot escape the local nature of our knowledge. But we can escape the error of believing that knowledge and ways of understanding acquired in a particular community are readily transferable and effortlessly acceptable to all others. By testing the propositions of one community against those of others, students can begin to grapple with one of the most important lessons of liberal learning: the contingency and the provisionality of much that we believe we know.

References

Association of American Colleges. *Integrity in the College Curriculum: A Report to the Academic Community.* Washington, D.C.: Association of American Colleges, 1985.

Association of American Colleges. Mission statement. Washington, D.C.: Association of American Colleges, 1989.

Association of American Colleges. *Liberal Learning and the Arts and Sciences Major.* Vol. 1: *The Challenge of Connecting Learning.* Washington, D.C.: Association of American Colleges, 1991.

Belenkey, M. F., Clinchy, B. M., Goldberger, N. R., and Tarule, J. M. *Women's Ways of Knowing: The Development of Self, Voice, and Mind.* New York: Basic Books, 1986.

Boyer, E. *College: The Undergraduate Experience in America.* New York: HarperCollins, 1987.

Curry, W., and Hager, E. "Assessing General Education: Trenton State College." In D. F. Halpern (ed.), *Student Outcomes Assessment: What Institutions Stand to Gain.* New Directions for Education, no. 59. San Francisco: Jossey-Bass, 1987.

Glaser, R. "Education and Thinking: The Role of Knowledge." *Educational Psychologist,* 1984, *39,* 93–104.

Pascarella, E. T., and Terenzini, P. T. *How College Affects Students: Findings and Insights from Twenty Years of Research.* San Francisco: Jossey-Bass, 1991.

Perkins, D. N., and Salomon, G. "Are Cognitive Skills Context-Bound?" *Educational Researcher,* Jan./Feb. 1989, pp. 16–25.

Resnick, L. B. "Learning in School and Out." *Educational Researcher,* Dec. 1987, pp. 13–20.

Rudolph, F. *Curriculum: A History of the American Undergraduate Course of Study Since 1636.* San Francisco: Jossey-Bass, 1977.

Russell, D. R. *Writing in the Academic Disciplines, 1970–1990: A Curricular History.* Carbondale: Southern Illinois University Press, 1991.

Voss, J. F., Greene, T. R., Post, T. A., and Penner, B. C. "Problem Solving Skill in the Social Sciences." In *The Psychology of Learning and Motivation: Advances in Research and Theory.* Vol. 17. New York: Academic Press, 1983.

CAROL GEARY SCHNEIDER is executive vice president of the Association of American Colleges and director of AAC's initiatives on revitalizing majors.

PART TWO

Proposals for Revitalizing the Arts and Sciences Major

*The American Association of Colleges' (AAC) analysis of the
major as liberal learning argues each major's obligation to serve as
a temporary learning community for its students, simultaneously
fostering focused inquiry and the capacity to engage in integrative
learning.*

Toward a Richer Vision:
The AAC Challenge

Carol Geary Schneider

The first chapters of this volume reviewed a series of issues that call into question the traditional equation of liberal arts or disciplinary majors with the liberating critical and analytical capacities so highly valued in our society as a hallmark of baccalaureate liberal education. At the least, the mounting critique of both the premises and practices that inform discipline-based majors suggests a need for a fresh review of the work of a liberal arts major as liberal learning. In 1988, the Association of American Colleges (AAC), a national society of more than six hundred public and private colleges and universities, initiated such a review. With support from the U.S. Department of Education Fund for the Improvement of Postsecondary Education and the Ford Foundation, the association worked in collaboration with task forces from twelve learned societies[1] to reexamine educational goals, and it recommended changes in arts and sciences majors in the context of a baccalaureate liberal arts degree. Ten of the participating learned societies assumed responsibility for analyzing the traditional disciplinary majors of biology, economics, history, mathematics, philosophy, political science, psychology, physics, sociology, and religion. Two other societies addressed interdisciplinary majors, one in a general report on interdisciplinary concentrations and one in a specific analysis of women's and gender studies. Findings from this initiative were published in the three-volume series *Liberal Learning and the Arts and Sciences Major* (Association of American Colleges, 1991a, 1991b, 1992).

In organizing this collaborative review of the arts and sciences major as liberal learning, a National Advisory Committee[2] framed the AAC charge to the task forces, which invited the working groups of the learned societies

NEW DIRECTIONS FOR HIGHER EDUCATION, no. 84, Winter 1993   © Jossey-Bass Publishers

to look at each major's goals for study in depth, sequential learning, and intellectual development; students' experiences of "connected learning"; and the educational implications of relations between different intellectual communities or fields (Association of American Colleges, 1991b). The charge cited the criticisms of the major that AAC had published earlier in *Integrity in the College Curriculum* (Association of American Colleges, 1985). It also proposed general directions for reform, suggesting that any major ought to be able to specify goals for students' introductory, intermediate, and advanced work, and that majors should designate strategies that encourage students to integrate their learning work within a field and across the curriculum (Association of American Colleges, 1991b). The committee further invited the task forces to examine topics they had identified as of interest to their respective fields. Although the charge did not cite the emerging literature that distinguishes well-structured from diffuse or would-be disciplines, the advisory committee did invite the task forces to question the future of discipline-based collegiate study, remarking that "there appears to be a growing sense, in many fields, that the customary disciplinary divisions are no longer self-evident. Customary boundaries are being erased, creating new disciplines and combinations of previously distinct disciplines. . . . How does this affect the way in which a major program structures its relations with other fields? . . . Ought there to be explicit occasions for students to reflect on competing claims of different fields? On connections across fields?" (Association of American Colleges, 1991b). The learned societies and their appointed task forces accepted the AAC charge as a broad framework for analysis, and twelve task forces appointed by the respective learned societies worked to examine their majors within the parameters set by AAC. AAC also organized a series of national conferences exploring purposes and practices in college majors, and beginning in 1990, many of the learned societies sponsored field-based discussions within their own national or regional meetings.

In 1991, AAC published executive summaries of the work of the twelve task forces as *Reports from the Fields* (Association of American Colleges, 1991b). Concurrently, each learned society published through its own channels the complete text of its analysis and recommendations to its members. Through dialogue with the learned societies, and with drafts of their reports in hand, AAC's National Advisory Committee developed a normative framework for liberal learning in majors, which was published as *The Challenge of Connecting Learning* (Association of American Colleges, 1991a). This framework builds on premises first offered in the AAC charge to the task forces, but *Challenge* goes beyond the charge to offer both a philosophical view of the liberal arts major and a set of broad organizing principles that all majors ought to meet, albeit in varying ways depending on their disciplinary traditions and institutional circumstances.

The Arts and Sciences Major as Liberal Learning

The liberal arts major, Challenge argues, rests its claims as liberal education not on the subject matter it teaches and not on conventional distinctions between disciplines and preprofessional studies but rather on the "intellectual habits fostered through and inseparable from successful completion of a course of study" (Association of American Colleges, 1991a, p. 3). While recognizing important cultural differences among academic fields, institutional missions, and student populations, Challenge nonetheless argues that shared liberal learning standards should guide all liberal arts programs in framing courses of study. The authors ground this claim, in part, on the learned societies' acceptance of the charge's conceptual premises as a framework for discussion of the major and, in part, on a reassertion of traditional claims that liberal education fosters a critical spirit and provides tools appropriate to critical inquiry. The authors further reflected the academic community's growing interest in confronting the fragmentation of the contemporary college education and the influence of feminist calls for decreasing the disjuncture between analytical and connected knowing (Belenkey, Clinchy, Goldberger, and Tarule, 1986).

In debating the propositions set forth in Challenge, members of the National Advisory Committee discussed extensively the enculturative view of learning in a disciplinary community (see Chapters One and Three). Although some committee members initially argued that the findings about enculturation were evidence that something new and deliberately interdisciplinary ought to replace the traditional major, the National Advisory Committee as a group eventually concluded that the social dimensions of the departmental major were an opportunity and an underused resource rather than a debilitating constraint. The departmental major, committee members became persuaded, ought to be envisioned as a learning community, a social and deliberately developmental context for collegiate learning. In short, the committee decided to build on the enculturative functions of interpretive communities rather than seek, futilely, as most committee members thought, to eliminate those communities. In principle, members of the committee argued in a series of animated discussions, the department ought to provide a "home" for students' intellectual development, a context in which all students can expect to find both mentors and mentoring. This intellectual home, Challenge suggests, should provide intellectual space and academic credit for students to both integrate and interrogate their progress as learners. Since faculty members and students are drawn to each department by some measure of common interests, the departmental major should be seen and managed as an intentional community, an organizing center designed to help students make educational and personal sense of their learning both within and beyond the academy. Challenge describes in considerable detail the practices that should characterize these homes or, more accurately, home bases for integrative learning and reflection on that learning.

Challenge presents proposals for the major as learning community under three organizing principles: curricular coherence, critical perspectives and connected learning. It also argues that departments must commit themselves to inclusiveness, reexamining under this last rubric each of the first three themes to show that constructive attention to coherence, critical perspective, and connected learning can also reduce educational barriers for those students who presently perceive arts and sciences study as irrelevant or even hostile to their perceived needs and interests.

Curricular Coherence

When the advisory committee first framed the AAC charge to the task forces, no part of it raised more questions among the learned societies than the suggestion that the major should concern itself with "sequential learning" (Association of American Colleges, 1991b). Given the academy's traditional equation of learning in a major with subject matter or subfield coverage, most of the task forces initially assumed that sequential learning must mean a sequential organization of content such as we find in physics or, to a lesser extent, in economics. To the scientists, as Stark and Lattuca suggest in Chapter Five, this proposal was congenial. To the humanists and most of the social sciences task forces, it was not. But the AAC National Advisory Committee had something broader in mind than what committee members also viewed as an anachronistic effort to identify educational sequences with course content.

The major, Challenge insisted, ought to have a beginning, a middle, and an end. Department faculty should know what entry-level courses in the major are introducing; they should know how middle-level work builds on and extends that introduction; and they should hold a discernible, explicit, and public understanding of what it means for a student to complete the work of the major. Such a sense of progression might, Challenge observed, be built on a base of less and more advanced content. But Challenge also noted numerous other ways of organizing an educationally developmental program of study: a program might organize study around problems or contested issues, or it might focus on teaching students to use the concepts and methods of the discipline itself. This proposal was extensively discussed by the National Advisory Committee and members of several task forces, and the report on the philosophy major from the task force of the American Philosophical Association provides an example of what disciplinary intentionality might mean in practice for a field whose teaching of content is traditionally eclectic or loosely structured. The philosophy report argues that there is no inherent distinction between introductory or advanced content in philosophy. Plato's Republic can be taught to novices, and it can be the subject of exquisitely advanced and specialized inquiry. Yet there are clear differences between the tasks appropriate to beginning and advanced students of philosophy. "Introductory work should intro-duce students to skills necessary for doing philosophy" (Association of Amer-ican Colleges, 1991b, p. 106). Intermediate courses should provide oppor-tunities for practicing these skills, which include, for example, recognizing a philosophical question, grasping a philosophical argument, engaging in philo-sophical discussion, and writing philosophical papers that use interpretation, argument, and library research. In advanced courses, students should be using these skills to make their own philosophical critiques; they should also be expected to reflect on and debate the nature of the discipline itself (pp. 106–107).

History department deliberations at Rowan College in New Jersey (for-merly Glassboro State College) provide another example of the same principle of sequential learning. As part of a general effort to strengthen their major pro-gram, faculty identified disciplinary tasks basic to historical analysis. They then proposed that each student should compile, across a course of study, a portfo-lio that demonstrates competence in such skills as writing a bibliographical interpretation, analyzing documentary evidence, and writing research papers based on primary sources. In both of these examples, students' actual choice and sequence of content might vary markedly within the department or across departments. What provides curricular coherence is the expectation that stu-dents should encounter opportunities, especially in middle-level courses, to practice disciplinary capabilities basic to their fields of study.

Majors as Learning Communities

As a way for departments to structure educational focus while retaining depart-mental autonomy in choice of content, Challenge's proposal that the major focus purposefully on students' sequential development of capacities for inquiry may seem inherently reasonable, perhaps even self-evident. However, departments have traditionally been viewed as educationally nondirective administrative structures. Behind Challenge's recommendations stands a revo-lutionary view of the department as a *deliberative* educational community. If curricular coherence is to become a reality, a new corporate ethos will have to undergird faculty's understanding of what students are supposed to accomplish in a program and faculty's collectively owned responsibility to help students accomplish curriculum goals. *Challenge* spends considerable time delineating this ethos:

• If the major is to offer an intentional educational experience, faculty members must agree collectively on goals for the major, ways of addressing those goals across the curriculum, and ways of assessing students' achievement of those goals.

• Since students differ markedly in their backgrounds, learning styles, and interests, faculty need to collectively address the ways goals for the major will "intersect with the varying needs of different students" (p. 7). Majors may, for

example, need to offer multiple entry points in order to appropriately serve
transfer students and underprepared students as well as traditional students.

• To fulfill their responsibility to teach the approaches and assumptions
of the field, faculty must "take collective responsibility for shaping a core set
of courses that . . . introduce the kinds of questions a field typically asks,
explore the ways it undertakes investigations, specify its frames of reference,
and expose its disputed issues" (p. 9).

• Since cafeteria-style study programs provide little opportunity for student dialogue, faculty ought to see that at least some "reasoned fraction" of a
program's offerings are taken by students in common.

• Since students in most programs will take much of their work in self-
determined selections of content and sequence, departments should provide
public opportunities for students to discuss their rationales for their programs,
including their choice of electives. These discussions ought to be reviewed by
faculty in order to compare students' rationales with faculty's shared understanding of what students are supposed to be doing.

• To facilitate students' integration of their work, major programs should
encourage such devices as reflective capstone seminars or intellectual autobi-
ographies in which students interpret the meaning and significance of their
learning to date. "Minimally, curricular space should be allotted for faculty-
student discussion of this integrating activity" (p. 11).

What these proposals challenge is the usual isolation from one another of
the various constituents of a major program: students from behind-the-scenes
scholarly debate and dialogue, faculty from colleagues' courses and students'
individual and corporate thinking about what to study and what they are
learning from their studies. As Challenge makes clear, to provide curricular
coherence, faculty need to become intentional and collaborative about the
ways in which their different courses and the general community culture support students' learning. In the departments envisioned by Challenge, faculty
may continue to teach the content of, for example, the Russian Revolution or
the African Diaspora in ways they judge appropriate. Simultaneously, however,
they assume responsibility for the department's shared goals when they decide
the kinds and levels of assignments students will complete within a course. If
students are to present document-based research papers as part of a graduation portfolio, some faculty will have to agree to teach them how to assess doc-
uments while others must teach them how to write a research paper. If, as the
task force report on the field of political science proposes, a major identifies
such concepts as power, justice, and law that all students should study before
graduation, both students and faculty must be able to discern the courses in
which these concepts are taught. These collective educational responsibilities
would no longer be, as so often they are now, the accidental sum of each faculty member's preference and private choice.

Robert Schoenberg (1993), one of Challenge's authors, has underlined
the centrality of this change in dialogue with institutions now working on
a subsequent AAC curriculum change initiative entitled "Re-Forming Arts

and Sciences Majors." When a department designates a subset of courses designed to deepen disciplinary proficiency (for example, methods, research, or capstone seminars), Schoenberg argues that "the department owns a piece of each of these courses: they are not the exclusive property of the faculty members teaching them" (p. 5). While faculty members frequently see the value of this idea in the abstract, Schoenberg observes, it almost always challenges actual departmental practices in fundamental and potentially revolutionary ways. And almost every department with whom he discusses this theme predicts that unspecified members "will never accept this" (p. 5).

Critical Perspective and Connected Learning

While Challenge's discussion of curricular coherence deliberately builds on the enculturative dimensions of learning in a major, Challenge's second and third organizing principles for liberal learning propose an equally deliberate counterpoint. The goal of curricular coherence is teaching students to work within the frame of an interpretive community. However, in marked contrast, Challenge's emphases on critical perspective and connected learning are intended to encourage the student to step outside that interpretive community, to view knowledge from a number of different perspectives including application and personal significance. It is in this stepping outside, Challenge implies, that the major meets the traditional standard for liberal education and teaches ways of knowing that question and challenge parochial certainties. No student, and no curriculum, can question every set of parochial assumptions. But every student can have at least one powerful experience of learning to critique the assumptions of an authorizing knowledge community. And only the major, which represents a primary commitment for both students and faculty, can make such an experience really count.

The major is not an end in itself, Challenge insists, nor is it best envisioned as a mini-preview of graduate education. For the most part, faculty should recognize that students "join the community of the major briefly; ultimately, they must disengage and leave" (p. 12). This point has normative as well as descriptive force: the major, Challenge argues, should be structured so that leaving it serves an educational function. "A student enters the 'home' offered by the major in order, finally, to be able to leave it and see it from the outside in, by taking the knowledge, experience, and wisdom gained therein and testing them against the perspectives of other fields and the challenges of the world outside" (p. 5). In short, the college education as liberal learning must challenge the inherent limitations, the inescapable parochialism of any specific community, including the disciplinary communities that form arts and sciences majors.

Critical perspectives and connected learning represent related but distinctive ways of challenging disciplinary limitations. Challenge suggests that courses that provide critical perspective should examine a field's presuppositions while experiences that foster connected learning ideally take the student not only beyond the field but even beyond the academy. The major, Challenge argues, should assume responsibility for helping students put together the different parts of their education: connecting general education and elective or cognate courses with learning in the major and juxtaposing academic studies with such off-campus learning as internships, fieldwork, or study abroad.

Disconnected Learning

In an informal survey[3] of more than one thousand arts and sciences students undertaken as part of its review of the major, AAC found that, for the most part, they "seldom" perceived any substantive connections between courses taken in the major and those taken in general education. With few exceptions, the students reported that they did not need to draw on knowledge (addressed in the survey as separate from skills) developed in courses outside their field to meet the expectations of their courses in the major. Yet faculty experimenting with oral examinations for a separate AAC project on assessment in the major have reported that students, when pressed on the sources of their oral answers, sometimes pointed to nonmajor courses as the basis for particular replies.

Speculating on the disparity between the survey data and the oral interview reports, AAC staff wondered whether the survey might be capturing what students assumed to be an ethic of separation between the major and general education; perhaps students thought their departments ought, as a matter of simple fairness, to make it possible to pass any particular course on the basis of material learned in that course alone. Perhaps students think it would be wrong to ground achievement in a specific course on learning from earlier courses, especially courses taken outside the major. Perhaps the variable sequences that so characterize U.S. higher education, at least in the humanities and social sciences, have unwittingly resulted in a belief that it is not worth even considering the idea that learning in those fields is developmental, recursive, or integrative. Large stacks of unretrieved papers and examination books to be found in every departmental office also strongly suggest that many students see their learning in any specific course as self-contained and unlikely to be needed in the future.

Certainly students can be forgiven if they innocently assume that U.S. colleges and universities do not value either integration or recursiveness as an integral dimension of higher learning. The modular structure of U.S. higher education, while allowing maximum flexibility to both students and faculty, makes it exceptionally difficult in most humanities and social sciences fields to take anything for granted about what a student knows in a field. Although many of the sciences have well-structured prerequisites, the humanities and social sciences frequently admit into advanced courses students with little or no background in the subject matter (Zemsky, 1989).

The sciences, while less culpable in mixing novice and more advanced students in the same courses, can successfully impart their own ethos of fragmentation to students, implicitly drawing a firm barrier between what they count as science and the messier world of values, social commitments, and implications. AAC's informal survey of students' experiences in arts and sciences majors asked a number of questions about connected learning including whether courses in the major helped students address what they saw as "important societal issues," "issues of personal significance," and "values issues." In general, science and mathematics students reported that their courses in the major did not typically make such connections. But five physics majors at one of the nation's most selective liberal arts colleges took the matter further. These five wrote a letter of protest to the survey's authors. The survey implied, these seniors indicated, that the major ought to address societal questions, values, or issues of personal significance. But none of these matters, they insisted, had anything to do with physics. All five were "A" students. All planned to attend graduate school in their field. And all five of these very able students had internalized, their letter suggests, a monastic perception that scientific knowledge is disconnected by definition from self, society, and societal values.

Connected Majors

Challenge's recommendations for fostering critical perspectives counter such intellectual monasticism. They eschew, however, the conventional campus effort to inoculate students against the major through a general education constituted on different premises from and competing with the major. Instead, the recommendations assign to the major itself an additional layer of social and educational responsibilities. These responsibilities include helping students learn to place their studies in context, and helping them learn, simultaneously, to value contextualization and its close ally interdisciplinary thinking. Just as learning to think within a discipline requires the student to become part of an intentional community, Challenge suggests, so helping students learn to think beyond a discipline is also a shared or corporate responsibility of that community.

• To develop critical perspective on their knowledge, Challenge says, students "must be willing to revise what they have held previously as certain . . . and they must engage in the kind of collaborative work in which they become open to criticism." But this can happen only if the student is part of "an academic community that sees as an important value of liberal learning bringing private precept into public discourse. . . . Faculty members must take seriously what students believe about a given subject and engage their prior knowledge so that new learning restructures the old, complicating and correcting it rather than merely living side by side with it" (Association of American Colleges, 1991a, pp. 12–13).

• To foster student and faculty rethinking of concepts and precepts, faculty must recognize an additional dimension of general education. Properly understood, general education emerges *from* specialized knowledge, complementing, restructuring, and complicating it. At the most sophisticated level, advanced work in the major ought to become general, or generalizing, education.

• Since academic credit is the academy's measure of value, departments must provide "curricular space and academic credit as well as persuasive guides and models" to help students cultivate critical perspective. "It is an iron law of education that students will neither criticize nor integrate what the faculty will not" (Association of American Colleges, 1991a, p. 14).

• To foster deep understanding of critical perspective, each major must open up its own contested issues, including the profound critiques of each field's founding premises that are emerging *from* scholarship in feminist, ethnic, and other critical studies. Not only the criticism but the issues at stake in the critiques should become matters of community debate and general dialogue.

• *Challenge's* recommendations for connected learning develop further this ethos of shared dialogue and collaborative inquiry, stating that, "while it is important for students to develop a detached critical perspective on subject matter, *it is equally important for them to care about subject matter and see its implications for the way they live their lives*" (Association of American Colleges, p. 16, emphasis added). Protesting the academy's habit of leaving implications and applications to each student's individual or extracurricular musings, *Challenge* calls for community attention to the major's significance for students viewed as social individuals, not just apprentice intellectuals. The major should help students think through the significance their learning has for other aspects of their lives by inviting students to work "in a setting that encourages collaboration in the exploration and reformulation of issues in relation to both academic inquiry and personal experience" (Association of American Colleges, 1991a, p. 16).

• To help students learn to value connecting learning, the major should care about students' narratives: stories that connect intellectual journeys with extracurricular, personal, and public learnings. "The accredited public space that ought to be provided for connecting learning should involve both faculty members and student peers in listening, valuing, and creatively engaging such stories" (Association of American Colleges, 1991a, p. 16).

For many students, *Challenge* recognizes, connecting learning must mean caring about the connections between what happens in school and their future lives in the work force. *Challenge's* authors did not recoil from this nontraditional linking of the liberal arts with vocations and translations to the world of work. In their discussion of inclusiveness, the authors point out that nontraditional and underrepresented students often enter the academy with practical and vocational interests and, therefore, are likely to shy away from the arts and sciences altogether. Departmental faculty who insist that learning is "valuable solely in itself, apart from (indeed, indifferent or hostile to) any practical applications" (p. 20), unwittingly reinforce the message that the arts and sciences are an exclusionary enclave, not really open to every student. The major that wishes to become an inclusive community will need to engage students' entirely reasonable assumption that college should provide them with useful and usable capacities.

In this context, Challenge might have considered more fully the emergent research concerning transfer, that is, the degree to which knowledge and procedures learned in one context can be transferred to another. Few issues are so central to the general claim that liberal learning provides a course for life; few are so underexplored by arts and sciences faculty.

Perkins and Salomon (1989) point out that, although learning seldom transfers automatically from one domain to another, students can be taught in ways that make transfer much more likely. Summarizing findings from a number of different studies, many of children, Perkins and Salomon point especially to the importance of teaching students to look at the underlying structures of problems in different domains and of teaching students to generate the rules that seem to govern particular categories of problems. Perhaps most importantly, they observe that transfer is enhanced when "learning takes place in a social context (e.g., reciprocal teaching), whereby justifications, principles, and explanations are socially fostered, generated and contrasted" (p. 22). Whether transfer occurs at all, they insist, is very much a matter of how the learning is structured.

What the transfer research implies is that critical perspectives and connecting learning are not elective dimensions of learning in a major. If faculty in each discipline believe, as most surely do, that their field provides illuminating lenses for the world, it seems to be through developing critical understanding and experimenting with deliberate translations that students best learn how to adjust those lenses in a variety of situations. As Stark and Latucca accurately remind us (Chapter Five), the intellectual frameworks of some disciplines make them less receptive than AAC might like to issues of critical perspective and integrative learning. Thus, the question for each field to explore is the degree to which its inherited traditions actually frustrate its espoused commitment to liberal education.

Liberal and Professional Majors

As I described in the introduction to this volume, the AAC study of the major addressed only liberal arts majors directly, contending that a review of the major as liberal learning ought to begin in domains that have traditionally owned liberal education—however they defined that term—as a central concern. However, the analysis of the major in The Challenge of Connecting Learning contains implications for liberal education in fields conventionally construed as professional. Challenge treats the enculturative aspects of disciplinary learning in ways broadly parallel to the educational approaches of professional studies. Both academic and professional fields own the goal of teaching students to use concepts and techniques or methods so they can identify, frame, and address complex problems. The chief real difference may be that most professional majors are more explicit about and better organized to achieve this goal than the typical humanities or social sciences major. (Mathematics and the sciences are typically more structured, although with large variations among both fields and institutions.)

What makes the liberal arts major liberal, Challenge suggests, is the introduction of complicating perspectives: issues, concepts, contexts, and critiques drawn from other frames of reference and from disputed positions within a field. Equally important to the major as liberal learning, says Challenge, are societal and personal considerations of significance. Implicit in Challenge's approach is a model that might be more fully explored for students in professional fields, who are now two-thirds of all college students. Conventionally, colleges and universities have regarded general education courses and requirements as the route to liberal learning for their professional students. In a more imaginative future, we may begin to ask whether professional majors and liberal arts majors should be equally able to integrate both contextualizing and critical perspectives within their programs. The business student may be asked to learn history and culture and to study both in ways that challenge some of the assumptions on which business is founded as a field. The economics student may be asked to develop a complementary concentration in psychology and history, again with the expectation that she will encounter in those subjects concepts and approaches that challenge the rationalist foundations of economics. The computer science student may be expected to take a set of specially designed courses in science, technology, and values designed to help him anticipate the significance of his technical knowledge to the world around him. All students may be expected to do internships and to integrate their experiential learning with their learning in their majors, through written reflections shared with mentors and student colleagues.

In short, in a more imaginative future, we may put aside the assumption that some fields convey liberal education by their ethos, subject matter, and inherited status in the academy, while others (which have most of the students) can aspire only to lesser intellectual standing. We may then take seriously the challenge to every major to become a community organized to involve both faculty and students in questioning, debating, and even revising their field's own founding assumptions.

Notes

1. The thirteen members of the National Advisory Committee were John W. Chandler, president emeritus, Association of American Colleges; Blythe Clinchy, professor of psychology, Wellesley College; Gerald Graff, professor of English, University of Chicago; William Scott Green, professor of religion, University of Rochester; Patrick J. Hill, professor of interdisciplinary studies, Evergreen State College; Jane Butler Kahle, professor of science education, Miami University

(Ohio); Priscilla Laws, professor of physics, Dickinson College; Paula McClain, professor of public affairs, University of Virginia; Yolanda T. Moses, president, City College, City University of New York; Hans Palmer, professor of economics, Pomona College; Robert Schoenberg, senior fellow, Association of American Colleges; Jonathan Z. Smith, Robert O. Anderson Distinguished Service Professor of the Humanities, University of Chicago; John A. Thorpe, provost for undergraduate education, Queens College, City University of New York.

2. The twelve participating learned societies were American Academy of Religion, American Association of Physics Teachers, American Economics Association, American Historical Association, American Institute of Biological Sciences, American Philosophical Association, American Political Science Association, American Psychological Association, American Sociological Association, Mathematical Association of America, National Women's Studies Association, Society for Values in Higher Education.

3. Because the students in this 1989 survey were not chosen at random, AAC used the survey only as an informal resource for the AAC National Advisory Committee and the task forces and did not publish the results.

References

Association of American Colleges. Integrity in the College Curriculum: A Report to the Academic Community. Washington, D.C.: Association of American Colleges, 1985.

Association of American Colleges. Liberal Learning and the Arts and Sciences Major. Vol. 1: The Challenge of Connecting Learning. Washington, D.C.: Association of American Colleges, 1991a.

Association of American Colleges. Liberal Learning and the Arts and Sciences Major. Vol. 2: Reports from the Fields. Washington, D.C.: Association of American Colleges, 1991b.

Association of American Colleges. Liberal Learning and the Arts and Sciences Major. Vol. 3: Program Review and Education Quality in the Major. Washington, D.C.: Association of American Colleges, 1992.

Belenkey, M. F., Clinchy, B. M., Goldberger, N. R., and Tarule, J. M. Women's Ways of Knowing: The Development of Self, Voice, and Mind. New York: Basic Books, 1986.

Perkins, D. N., and Salomon, G. "Are Cognitive Skills Context-Bound?" Educational Researcher, Jan./Feb. 1989, pp. 16–25.

Schoenberg, R. Unpublished report on visits to eight institutions working on restructuring major programs, Association of American Colleges, Washington, D.C., Jan. 1993.

Zemsky, R. Structure and Coherence: Measuring the Undergraduate Curriculum. Washington, D.C.: Association of American Colleges, 1989.

CAROL GEARY SCHNEIDER is executive vice president of the Association of American Colleges and director of AAC's initiatives on revitalizing majors.

Faculty respond to suggestions for curricular change in ways
that reflect their disciplinary perspectives. Faculty from varied
disciplines, therefore, will need thoughtful leadership to develop
support for a common curricular framework.

Diversity Among Disciplines: The Same Goals for All?

Joan S. Stark, Lisa R. Lattuca

The proposals of the Association of American Colleges (AAC) for revitalizing majors are part of a larger higher education reform movement that has articulated concerns about undergraduate education since the 1970s. As a voice for reform within the higher education community, AAC has been proactive and positive in its approach, engaging faculty task forces to tackle specific problems of undergraduate education. The solicitation of faculty opinions and ideas and the direct involvement of faculty in proposals for change make the AAC-inspired recommendations potentially powerful influences on faculty thinking about the curriculum. As described in Chapter Four, a recent AAC project focused the attention of twelve learned society task forces, composed of teacher/scholars in selected liberal arts disciplines, on the challenge of improving the undergraduate major in their respective fields. Our interest in curriculum development and planned educational change led us to view these reports as potential indicators of broader faculty thinking about the college curriculum. Since the task forces represented specific disciplinary viewpoints, we wondered whether each group's ability and willingness to address the challenge to improve the undergraduate major would differ along disciplinary lines, as previous research we review later in this chapter would suggest. To explore disciplinary influences on the ways the task forces responded to the challenge, we made two separate content analyses of ten of the disciplinary reports published in *Reports from the Fields* (Association of American Colleges, 1991b). (Because we wished to concentrate on the disciplines, we did not analyze the reports from the two interdisciplinary fields that also took part in the AAC review of college majors.) Through these analyses, we hoped to discern patterns of response that would demonstrate both the extent to which each field addressed

NEW DIRECTIONS FOR HIGHER EDUCATION, no. 84, Winter 1993 © Jossey-Bass Publishers

the charge as stated by AAC and the influence of disciplinary perspectives on each task force's proposals for change in the major.

In the first of our analyses, we identified patterns in each task force's direct responses to the four-part challenge, outlined by AAC in The Challenge of Connecting Learning (Association of American Colleges, 1991a). AAC had challenged each field to increase its major's capacity for achieving curricular coherence, developing students' critical perspective, connecting students' learning with other fields and with students' lives, and including underrepresented students. In the second analysis, we examined the task force reports for mentions of curricular concerns, ideas, and issues that were incidental to the charge, that is, points that were not made in direct response to the AAC Charge to the Task Forces but that could be assumed to represent emergent concerns of the fields.

In our direct content analysis, the coding categories were predetermined; they represented the responses of the task forces to each element of the AAC challenge itself. In contrast, the second analysis did not employ predetermined categories; instead, the categories emerged as we recorded and coded the words, phrases, and sentences that discussed additional faculty concerns and ideas that the task forces seemed to need to express. In each of the content analyses, the coding of the reports followed essentially the same four-step process. After coding two sample task force reports to resolve differences in interpretation and ensure high reliability, two coders coded and cross-checked phrases, sentences, and groups of sentences in the remaining reports. Thus, the crucial difference between the two processes was the definition of the coding categories, one predetermined and one emerging from the discourse itself. A second important difference, related to the first, occurred during the analysis stage. While the direct content analysis required us to identify responses to the four elements of the AAC framework, the analysis of unsolicited comments required us to associate the emerging categories into broader conceptual groupings, considering themes that might encompass and describe the categories. The groupings we developed reflected the reports' unsolicited emphases on disciplinary influences, institutional contexts, curricular design, and pedagogical strategies.

Before describing our comparisons of the disciplines' direct and unsolicited responses to the AAC challenge, we offer a brief review of the theory and research relevant to our discussion of disciplinary influences on the curriculum.

Disciplinary Influences on Curricula:
Theory and Research

Early theoretical and practical discussions of disciplinary differences have suggested several directions for research into the disciplinary influences on academic tasks such as curriculum reform. Kuhn (1970) theorized that different disciplines employ different cognitive frameworks and, therefore, differ not only in the way they make generalizations but also in the sets of exemplars they use to illustrate their generalizations and in the way the generalizing and the exemplars are related. He also argued that disciplines are characterized by the existence (in varying degrees) of paradigms that specify appropriate problems for study and appropriate methods for studying those problems. In fields like the physical sciences, these paradigms are highly developed; in fields like the humanities and social sciences, they are less well developed.

Using a sample of faculty from eighty university departments, Lodahl and Gordon (1972) tested Kuhn's thesis that paradigms are more developed in the physical sciences than the social sciences. The faculty's patterns of response tended to support Kuhn's concept of paradigm; physical sciences faculty reported more consensus on course content in undergraduate survey courses and in graduate-level offerings than social sciences faculty. The existence of greater or lesser paradigm development also influenced faculty respondents' attitudes and behaviors related to both teaching and research. Lodahl and Gordon concluded that well-developed paradigms facilitate teaching and research activities by offering more structure, and thus more predictability, than the less well developed paradigms.

Building on the earlier work of Phenix (1986), Dressel and Marcus (1982) described a discipline as a systematic way of organizing and studying phenomena. In their view, every discipline is composed of five components: the substantive component (assumptions, variables, concepts, principles, and relationships); the linguistic component (the symbolism through which elements are identified and relationships defined and explored); the syntactical component (the searching and organizing process around which the discipline develops); the value component (commitments about what is worth study and how it should be studied); and the conjunctive component (the relation to other disciplines). The interaction of these components gives each discipline its distinctive character. Research on these components has revealed important differences in the way disciplines structure knowledge (Donald, 1983, 1990), in faculty behaviors and attitudes related to course planning (Stark and others, 1988; Stark and others, 1990), and in the cognitive and social patterns that distinguish academicians in different fields (Becher, 1989).

In an effort to identify the differences that distinguish paradigmatic and nonparadigmatic disciplines, Biglan (1973a) asked faculty members at two institutions (a large university and a small liberal arts college) to judge similarities among areas of study. This research on the characteristics of subject matter in different academic areas led him to conclude that the three most important dimensions of any discipline's "cognitive style" were the extent to which a paradigm exists, the degree of concern with application, and concern with life systems (as opposed to nonlife systems).

Biglan (1973b) studied the effects of disciplines on social interactions; in contrast, Kolb (1981) investigated individual learning styles. Based on psychometric tests that measured preference for learning along two dimensions (abstract-concrete and active-reflective) in a large sample of practicing managers and graduate students in management, Kolb's findings largely mirrored those of Biglan. Kolb found that variations in learning styles were strongly associated with individuals' undergraduate educational experience, namely, their undergraduate major (Kolb, 1976). These learning style preferences remained highly stable from an individual's early years to adulthood. Moreover, the mapping of academic disciplines revealed considerable overlap between the classifications derived by Biglan and the clustering of data on the learning style dimensions of abstract-concrete and reflective-active (Kolb, 1981).

Comparing and combining the contributions of scholars like Kuhn, Biglan, and Kolb, Becher (1989) summarized the major subject matter distinctions among the general categories of knowledge found in the literature. Hard, pure knowledge (the domain of the natural sciences), he concluded, is marked by relatively steady cumulative growth. In these domains, knowledge is typically accrued in a linear fashion. He contrasted this growth by accretion to the predominantly recursive or reiterative pattern of development that characterizes the soft knowledge domains such as the social sciences and the humanities. Becher adopted the terms hard and soft from Biglan's classification system, but other scholars have suggested different descriptive terms. Toulmin (1972), for example, talked about "compact," "diffuse," and "would-be disciplines." In this typology, sciences might be described as compact disciplines, the social sciences as diffuse disciplines, and fields that are still in the developmental stages as "would-be" disciplines.

Noting that some of the more fundamental distinctions among disciplines are manifested through the medium of language, Becher adapted the classification system based on organizational strategies and research paradigms developed by Biglan and the learning styles preferences identified by Kolb. He used two of Biglan's classifications—the hard versus soft dimension, which places disciplines and fields on a continuum according to the degree to which they are paradigmatic,[1] and the pure versus applied dimension, which differentiates fields based on their concern with the application of knowledge. He also employed Kolb's two dimensions (abstract-concrete and active-reflective), claiming that these overlap considerably with the classifications developed by Biglan. Becher's model therefore juxtaposed a concrete/applied to hard/pure dimension against a reflective/hard to active/soft dimension. Becher argued that these dimensions, while they may not exhaust all the possible ways of classifying fields, are generally useful in distinguishing fields from one another.

Donald (1983) observed that conceptual structures in college courses varied by discipline. Science courses tended to be tightly structured with highly related concepts and principles while social science courses tended to be more loosely structured, with key concepts acting as organizers, and humanities courses tended to have open structures, less dependent upon either organizing strategies or concept interrelatedness. In later studies, Donald discovered that, beyond their differences in conceptual structure, the disciplines used distinguishable truth and validation strategies to determine the worthiness of new knowledge (1990) and that professors in different disciplines employed different methods to develop their students' ability to think (1992).

In a series of interview and survey studies of college-level course planning, Stark and others (1988, 1990) found strong correlations among faculty's background and preparation, views of their disciplines, beliefs about the educational purposes of college, and identification of influences that they believed affected how they planned and sequenced course content. In Stark's model of influences on course planning, such contextual factors as college goals, student characteristics, available services, and student goals are notably less influential on instructors than are instructors' beliefs about education and their disciplinary training and background. As we approached Reports from the Fields, we wondered whether groups of faculty responsible for a major program would also approach the task of curricular revision and redesign in ways that reflected their disciplinary training and beliefs.

Meeting the AAC Challenge

Analysis of disciplinary discourse reveals a discipline's cultural features, including differences from other disciplines in the way arguments are typically generated, developed, and reported and the work of peers is evaluated (Becher, 1987). As we described earlier, to examine the related question of how disciplinary perspectives influence curricular reform, we documented and described the arguments in the reports of ten disciplinary task forces as they answered the AAC challenge.[2] The traditional liberal arts disciplines represented were biology, economics, history, mathematics, philosophy, physics, political science, psychology, religion, and sociology. To facilitate discussion, we grouped these into three familiar categories: natural sciences (biology and physics) and mathematics, social sciences (economics, political science, psychology, and sociology), and humanities (history, philosophy, and religion).

In our analyses, we observed substantial variations in the ways the disciplinary groups addressed each component of the challenge and in the issues they discussed that did not refer to any specific element of the charge. These variations were consistent with past research on disciplinary differences. Following a summary of the AAC charge, we will discuss the task forces' direct responses first (organized by the three discipline groups just described) and then the unsolicited concerns and ideas.

The AAC Charge

AAC charged the researchers to focus on curricular coherence, students' critical perspective, connecting learning, and inclusiveness.

Curricular Coherence. The first element of the AAC charge challenged the faculty who made up each task force to develop a shared understanding of what study in depth in their field should accomplish and to suggest designs for coherent programs of study. The faculty were to set goals for student achievement, design a curriculum that encourages attainment of these goals, and develop ways of ensuring that the goals will be communicated to students and of assessing the degree to which the goals are achieved. AAC made clear that it viewed curricular coherence as the sequential organization of learning, and it challenged the faculty to develop a core of courses that establishes an intellectual agenda for majors. Finally, the AAC challenge asserted the responsibility of the faculty to make the structure, organization, and intent of the major clear to students, so that students can understand how particular courses contribute to their total educational experience.

Critical Perspective. AAC asserted that development of students' critical perspective requires that students become open to criticism, challenge their own views, and become willing to revise what they had assumed was certain. Students must encounter the limitations of their own learning communities and explore possibilities beyond those communities. To develop students' critical perspective, faculty must provide students with sufficient confidence in the discourses of their fields that the students can ask sophisticated questions about those fields. Faculty must also engage students' prior knowledge so that new learning restructures the old. Faculty should avoid the pitfall of relativism, teaching students instead to discriminate between viewpoints and discern when and for whom an issue or argument is valid. An additional faculty responsibility is to join disparate cross-disciplinary points of view, in order to foster students' critical perspective.

Connected Learning. AAC identified two usages of the term connected learning. First, the term can refer to the "capacity for constructing relationships among various modes of knowledge and curricular experiences" (Association of American Colleges, 1991a, p. 14). This is the capacity to apply learning from one context to another context. Second, the term can refer to the capacity to relate academic learning to the wider world, public issues, and personal experiences. In either case, connected learning is generalized learning, that is, it extends beyond the boundaries of the major. Thus, faculty were to design a major that encourages students to test the assumptions and proposals of their fields against their own experiences and helps students understand the frames of reference used in other fields.

Inclusiveness. Finally, AAC asked faculty to examine each field's obstacles to the participation of underrepresented students, and to work to eliminate those barriers. The faculty were asked to question the use of introductory courses as gatekeeping devices to exclude students who do not fit traditional expectations, and faculty were to adjust the content of the major to provide multiple entry points for students. AAC also stressed the desirability of communal learning in the major, suggesting that the major serve as an academic home where students participate in collaborative inquiry with their peers and with faculty who are charged with fostering students' intellectual and personal development.

Task Force Responses

The different task forces did respond differently when they considered the degree to which their disciplines already met the four challenges and devised ways to meet the challenges more fully (see the summary in Table 5.1).

Natural Sciences and Mathematics. All three of the sciences and mathematics task forces noted the typical uniformity of their curricula across institutions and reported that faculty in these disciplines had a high level of consensus about educational content and process. This uniformity aided the task forces in the natural and physical sciences in addressing the task of integrating knowledge and skills in their courses and programs. Each was able to

Table 5.1 Summary of Direct Responses to AAC Charge

	Science and Mathematics	Social Sciences	Humanities
Curricular coherence and coherent design	Readily addressed integration of knowledge and skills; advocated capstone courses and experiences.	Felt coherence to be problematic; content is eclectic, but coherence can be enhanced.	Gave a mixed response: some objected to or avoided idea; some attempted to meet challenge.
Goals	Stressed need for local department variation and autonomy.	Stressed need for local department variation and autonomy.	Stressed need for local department variation and autonomy.
Sequential learning	Found it possible to sequence; some fields have natural sequences.	Saw sequential learning as unfamiliar, but potentially possible.	Raised objections to prescribed sequences.
Critical perspective	Were unfamiliar with concept but having a fairly common belief in scientific method as primary perspective.	Addressed in varying ways: felt it was important; diverse approaches acceptable.	Stressed this perspective and linked with cultural and humanistic sensitivity; saw importance of context.
Connecting learning with other fields, life, and career	Were critical of fields' efforts to help students connect.	Were somewhat confident that connections are made across disciplines. Gave few specifics.	Gave a mixed response; assumed emphasis on connectedness.
Inclusiveness	Believed fields should be more open to students with diverse preparation; emphasized pedagogy.	Suggested altering content rather than pedagogy.	Stressed inclusiveness in terms of course content and learning environments.

suggest specific strategies for enhancing curricular coherence. The mathematics and sciences task forces were also consistent in emphasizing the goal of teaching students the concepts and principles of the disciplines. Thus, these task forces viewed as reasonable and accessible the AAC recommendation that learning in the major be sequenced. The physics task force viewed its discipline as inherently sequenced while the biology task force noted that course sequences are reflections of the background, training, and interests of the faculty. However, the perceived advantages of sequencing (for example, coherence) were also acknowledged as an obstacle to inclusiveness, putting underrepresented students at a disadvantage because such students come to college with diverse backgrounds, abilities, and interests. The task forces observed that many underrepresented students do not succeed in introductory science and math courses, which typically depend on previously acquired reasoning skills. The sciences and mathematics task forces also ran into difficulties when devising ways to develop critical perspectives in student majors. While the task forces recognized that their curricula as currently organized and taught did little to foster students' critical perspective, they offered only broad suggestions for integrating critical perspectives into courses or programs. Our content analysis revealed that these task forces tended to espouse the goal of learning concepts, facts, and principles over such goals as developing critical perspective. Despite the claims of a high degree of faculty consensus on content and methods, the sciences and mathematics task forces were reluctant to discuss specific goals for a coherent curriculum. Instead, they preferred that departments be given autonomy to devise goals compatible with each department's educational mission and student population.

Our analysis of unsolicited comments was consistent with our analysis of responses to the charge, since we found that discussion of teaching in the sciences reports emphasized specific pedagogical styles rather than specific techniques. Student research opportunities, for example, were given high priority as a general strategy, and active learning was viewed as appropriate primarily for laboratory rather than traditional classroom settings. Modes of instruction, such as laboratory sessions, are well entrenched and seemed to be considered givens by the sciences task forces. In their unsolicited comments, these task forces were especially concerned with contextual factors, which they believed affected their ability to design effective curricula. External influences, such as students' prior preparation for college-level work and the effect of graduate programs on undergraduate curricula, were seen as threats to the existing high level of consensus on curricular content and design. The sciences task forces were also self-critical about their major programs' ability to help students connect their learning to their lives. These acknowledgements, however, seemed to focus more on disciplinary structure and program design than on faculty's ability to teach students how to make connections.

Social Sciences. Coherence was a more difficult challenge for the social sciences than for the natural sciences. Social sciences task forces typically relied upon epistemological explanations for their curricular designs. In these fields, where alternative paradigms often compete, the task forces devoted considerable discussion to disciplinary characteristics, noting the diversity of programs, courses, and content. In particular, the less paradigmatic social sciences fields (sociology and psychology) repeatedly noted their lack of consensus on methods. However, the diversity of methodologies was not necessarily viewed as detrimental to students or the curriculum. Rather, as the political science task force noted, the acceptance of diverse methodologies is consistent with the liberal arts tradition, and in particular, conforms to AAC's definition of a liberal education. The exception to this pattern was the economics task force, which paid little attention to disciplinary divisions and appeared more certain of the types and boundaries of methods of inquiry in its field. This is consistent with Becher's observation (1989) that among the social sciences and humanities fields, economics and history resemble the natural sciences in their high level of internal agreement on principles and methods. The diversity of programs, courses, and methods in social sciences curricula may be the reason these task forces (except for economics) reported somewhat ambivalent discussions about sequential learning. While the task forces recommended that some sequencing be introduced, their discussions seemed to be intended to educate faculty rather than to express strong support for the concept. Sequential learning was generally perceived to be an unfamiliar organizing scheme. The acceptance of great diversity was also reflected in the reports' agreement that individual departments should retain autonomy in articulating curricular goals. In this regard, the social sciences were similar to the natural sciences. Although their fields were characterized by less diversity in programs and curricula, the natural sciences task forces nonetheless advocated departmental autonomy in setting curricular goals.

However, the social sciences task forces were more successful than those in the natural sciences in addressing the challenge of fostering students' critical perspective, variously interpreting this fostering as a process of intellectual development through which students become members of a disciplinary community, a process that maximizes students' capacities to analyze and interpret events, or a process through which students become aware of diverse approaches to study in their field and the limitations of the field's prevailing paradigms. Whereas the natural sciences task forces stressed concept learning as a primary goal of the major program, the social sciences closely linked concept learning with developing effective thinking skills. The social sciences faculty tended to argue that students must learn how to reason critically and analyze information, to reflect on their experiences, to struggle with ambiguity and to ask sophisticated questions about content and methodology. The social sciences task forces were also more confident than the mathematics and natural sciences task forces of their ability to help students make connections across disciplines and with their prior knowledge and their lives outside the academy. Interestingly, the social sciences' student-centered pattern of response was not as clear in the task force discussions of inclusiveness. Here the social sciences task forces responded to the increasing diversity of the student population with suggestions for altering program content rather than pedagogy or learning environments. The psychology task force alone suggested that faculty must become more responsive to different ways of knowing and discourse. It recommended that faculty continually renew their craft by exploring such pedagogical issues as how students learn most effectively.

The social sciences task forces focused their unsolicited commentary largely on choice of pedagogical activities, emphasizing a student-centered approach. This approach, in contrast to the natural sciences' subject matter orientation, resulted in an emphasis on active learning. The social sciences task forces advocated that passive-learning formats, such as lectures, be modified through the incorporation of such components as classroom discussions, senior-year theses, out-of-class activities, practicums, projects, and exercises in problem solving and decision making. In general, these task forces equated good teaching with the active involvement of students in the classroom.

The social sciences also stressed traditional liberal arts outcomes. While the natural sciences emphasized developing students' research skills, the social sciences viewed research skills as far less important than skills in oral and written communication, critical reading and lifelong learning, and effective thinking. Sociologists and psychologists asserted that the major should foster personal growth by addressing questions of ethics and values. Although the task forces' unsolicited comments noted the influence of external factors such as student heterogeneity on the major curriculum, these external pressures received far less emphasis than in the natural sciences. Instead, the department faculty's influence on the major program was seen as a more pressing concern. Three of the four social sciences task forces clearly asserted that goals and outcomes of the major program must be consistent with local missions and goals.

Humanities. As in the social sciences, the existence of alternative paradigms within individual humanities disciplines led the task forces to devote much discussion to the nature of their disciplines while noting the diversity of programs available to students. The responses of the humanities task forces to the goal of curricular coherence were correspondingly mixed. The philosophy task force suggested principles of coherence that were not based on content while the religion task force called for a progressively more advanced program, recognizing that sequencing could be accomplished in a number of ways. Only history, which we have already noted can be viewed as more paradigmatic than the other humanities, had a task force that directly addressed the AAC charge to design a coherent curriculum, although the task force did not equate coherence with sequential learning. The task force was clear that there simply is no prescribed sequence of courses or content in this field. This call for local autonomy in the development of curricula was echoed by every task force that answered the AAC charge. The humanities task forces also echoed those of the social sciences in observing a lack of consensus on research methodologies and in calling, in particular, for reflection on all possible methods although some humanities task forces tried to justify the predominant methods of their fields.

The humanities task forces readily addressed the goal of developing students' critical perspective. Two themes were evident: students were to be made aware of contextual boundaries, temporal and geographical, and were thought to need sensitivity, in addition to a critical eye, in exploring varying cultural perspectives. Both the history and religion task forces also noted the traditional appreciation in the liberal arts for contexts and traditions, human values, and the extent to which knowledge of the world is socially constructed. The task forces stressed that these perspectives, as well as certain skills (for example, research skills), are applicable in a wide range of contexts. In keeping with their focus on critical perspectives, the humanities task forces especially emphasized the development of effective thinking skills over concept learning. The development of other liberal arts skills, such as oral and written communication, critical reading, and lifelong learning, was also considered a primary goal of the major. Pedagogical decisions about course form were closely linked to these program objectives.

Both the history and philosophy task forces considered connecting learning a familiar theme. The connections they discussed often focused on integrating classroom work with students' lives, but the task forces also emphasized that study in their fields was enhanced when students were able to make connections with studies in other disciplines. Such integration, the humanities task forces believed, places these fields within a coherent vision of the liberal arts. The humanities' familiarity with connecting learning may have contributed to the task forces' ability to address the goal of inclusiveness. Comments on this latter goal stressed the need to offer multicultural perspectives in the major but also emphasized the importance of supportive learning environments for underrepresented students.

Among the unsolicited comments, the influence of faculty interests on departmental curricula was a prominent topic. The humanities task forces argued that major programs should capitalize on the competencies and interests of faculty because the programs will be stronger if faculty are able to teach in their areas of expertise. Furthermore, the limitations imposed by faculty competence must be also considered in designing the major program. In this way, the humanities—and social sciences—task forces emphasized internal constraints rather than external influences, as did the natural sciences and mathematics task forces.

Shared Concerns. While many issues and themes expressed in the task force reports clearly reflected specific disciplinary perspectives, two concerns were shared by all the disciplines: the plight of the nonmajor and the place of the major in a liberal arts education. Several of the fields (sociology, history, mathematics, biology, and religion especially) discussed the service function they provide to their institutions, noting that they often provide courses to students from other majors who must fulfill core or cognate course requirements.

Sociology and mathematics in particular observed that even in advanced courses in these fields, many students are not departmental majors. Several of the task forces were clearly worried about the quality of these courses for non-majors, both the nonmajor enrolled in general education courses provided by the department and those in other service courses that attract large numbers of nonmajors. The biology task force, for example, argued that if departments cannot do a better job of meeting the needs of nonmajors, separate courses must be developed. These courses should not be watered-down versions of courses for students who major in the field. The mathematics task force asserted that math departments must take seriously the need to provide the appropriate mathematical depth to nonmajors.

Discussion of the place of the major within the liberal arts curriculum also crossed disciplinary boundaries as several fields noted the need to integrate the disciplines and thereby provide a coherent vision of the liberal arts. As has been noted, many of the task forces (history, religion, political science, sociology, and mathematics) argued that their respective majors contributed strongly to this overall vision of coherence by cultivating general intellectual capacity and a variety of liberal arts skills. The history task force even recommended that if the institution does not incorporate the essential elements of liberal learning into its general offerings, history faculty should build these into the history curriculum and its offerings to nonmajors. Similarly, the biology task force suggested that faculty who present a negative picture of their institution's general education program to students limit the potential for those students' intellectual growth. At least some disciplines appeared to view as counterproductive the kinds of artificial divisions discussed in the Editors' Notes between learning in the major and learning in the general education program. These fields appear willing to accept responsibility for fostering a broad range of student learning outcomes not only those considered strictly relevant to the major program.

Implications for Curricular Reform

Our analysis of the task force reports in Reports from the Fields indicates that faculty question, albeit indirectly, whether a common view of teaching and learning is possible or appropriate. The reports demonstrate that faculty do not unanimously support the curricular changes espoused by AAC, or at least not in the words used in Challenge. Indeed, the current ability of the disciplines to simultaneously accommodate critical perspective, curricular coherence, and connecting learning appears limited.

We believe that the faculty on the task forces responded in good faith to the AAC charge but experienced difficulties, especially when disciplinary mantles needed to be shared or shed. In particular, the challenge of developing coherent curricula was seen as more attainable for the natural sciences, which view their fields as inherently sequenced and logical, than for the more diffuse disciplines. Faculty in the humanities and most social sciences fields did not easily agree on definitions of coherence, nor were they willing to assert that specified sequences of content were appropriate for their students. In contrast, the challenge to develop students' critical perspective was more readily addressed by the social sciences and humanities. The AAC definition of critical perspective viewed knowledge as contextual and concerned with broad dimensions of human experience. This focus is familiar to humanities and social sciences faculty and congruent with the strong emphasis they place on contingency and on fostering students' intellectual and personal development. In the natural sciences, the quantifiable nature of the phenomena under study, highly developed methods of inquiry, and consensus on validation criteria render the need for critical perspective less central. While the concept of coherence focuses attention on the structure of the discipline and its courses and program, the concept of critical perspective focuses attention on the development of student capabilities, including the capacity to look critically at one's own discipline. The sciences generally seek to enhance students' intellectual growth by developing students' capacity to use an accepted scientific perspective while the social sciences and humanities hope to encourage development by inviting students to debate varied perspectives.

Finally, while the humanities and social sciences task forces were comfortable interpreting the challenge of connecting learning, the sciences seemed to give connectedness far less attention. From the scientists' disciplinary perspective, the important connections for undergraduates may be those among the principles and concepts within each science itself rather than connections with the external world or with other disciplines. As the mathematics task force indicated, internal connections (classified by AAC under the challenge of coherence rather that of connecting learning) abound within the hard disciplines. Yet such connections are not always apparent to undergraduates. Faculty in these knowledge areas believe that connections with other fields occur later in a student's education; only students who have pursued advanced study, mastered a hierarchically structured knowledge base, and understand how scientific phenomena are interrelated are ready to link these phenomena with the social world (Becher, 1989).

The difficulty of translating the seemingly feasible AAC charge into recommendations acceptable to faculty in the various disciplines was highlighted when we looked at the task forces' unsolicited commentary. These discussions, which covered such areas as disciplinary characteristics and methodologies, pedagogical traditions, and educational purposes, revealed the depth of difference between many of the liberal arts fields under examination. The discussions also reflected the fields' different sensitivities to external and institutional influences and demands. It may come as a surprise to many that arts and sciences fields, which historically have been viewed as sharing certain philosophical perspectives pertaining to liberal education, fail to agree on what constitutes a good major. Yet earlier research findings clearly indicate that the influence of disciplinary training is among the strongest influences on course planning (Stark and others, 1990). Given the strong epistemological bases for many of the views expressed in these task force reports, it seems that these disciplinary influences also operate powerfully at the program-planning level. However, observers of faculty meetings in liberal arts colleges where vigorous debate about the shape of the collegewide curriculum is often heard will not be surprised.

Curricular reform is not, however, doomed to failure because of these deeply rooted differences. Our analysis suggests that when external forces are powerful enough, the disciplines appear able to look beyond their traditional perspectives and adjust. Like our earlier study of factors that affect course planning (Stark and others, 1990), our analysis of the task force reports demonstrated that environmental factors affected the disciplines in different ways, modifying the disciplines' influence on pedagogical decisions. For example, in disciplines with significant general education service obligations, pedagogical issues were emphasized more strongly than in fields with limited enrollments of nonmajors. In the fields with general education obligations, practical concerns superseded disciplinary perspectives, encouraging, for example, the mathematics task force to devote much of its report to discussion of creating learning environments, enhancing student confidence, and cultivating effective teaching styles. External influences may be stronger inducements to faculty to share perspectives than are internal challenges or reports.

The assumptions some faculty and administrators hold about the relative worth of the various disciplines may be another hurdle curriculum reform efforts must overcome. Since Kuhn (1970) suggested that the social sciences were in a pre-paradigmatic stage of development, there has been much debate about whether stronger paradigms should be equated with intellectual value and merit. Anecdotal evidence suggesting the power of this assumption is reflected in the familiar hierarchy at some colleges and universities: the natural sciences are at the top, followed by the social sciences, closely followed by the humanities. However, the educational significance of paradigm development may depend on what one is trying to achieve. We found that, although the highly paradigmatic fields can be successful in designing coherent curricula, they may have difficulty fostering students' critical perspective—a traditional and respected goal of a liberal arts education. In contrast, the less well developed social sciences, although they have trouble agreeing on curricular content and methods, are able to devise curricula that encourage the development of critical perspective. How does one balance these apparent advantages and disadvantages of high and low paradigm development? Is coherence more important than critical perspective? What is the relative value of connecting students' learning to their lives or of reducing barriers to underrepresented students? A person's answers to these questions will undoubtedly differ based on which educational outcomes or purposes he or she considers most worthwhile. Since the different disciplines place different values on specific educational purposes and student outcomes, clear consensus among the disciplines, and perhaps even among faculty from the same discipline, appears improbable if not patently impossible. Yet a liberal arts major, as envisioned by AAC, includes all these views—curricular coherence, critical perspective, and connecting learning. Possibly, it is less essential that each field reach the same consensus about the application of these educational principles than it is that students' education include experiences in each.

The lessons to be learned from the AAC exploration of the major are useful ones. Our analysis of faculty response to the call for curricular change indicates that change may be easier when the need for it is perceived as emanating from real, rather than philosophical, positions or needs. Without clear indicators that students or programs will suffer if change is not accomplished, faculty may not be inclined to substantially revise their thinking about either their curricula or disciplinary perspectives. Calls for reform based on lofty educational principles may not be as well received, or as quickly acted upon, as those based on immediate practical challenges. Furthermore, curricular reform advocates, both in higher education associations and on individual campuses, must consider the separate and powerful disciplinary perspectives of faculty involved in curricular reform. Simply acknowledging that such disciplinary influences exist is not sufficient; concerted efforts to find areas of agreement and compromise must be sought.

Notes

1. This dimension closely resembles the definition of a paradigm articulated by Thomas Kuhn (1970). According to Kuhn, the maturity of a field is based on the existence of one or more paradigms and the nature of these paradigms. Paradigms in mature disciplines and fields provide investigators or practitioners with the tools and techniques to study difficult problems with a greater guarantee of success because the paradigms supply methods and clues as part of the problem.
2. The results of the two content analyses we conducted are discussed more thoroughly in two separate papers. See Lattuca and Stark (in press) for the results of the direct content analysis and Lattuca and Stark (1993) for the results of the analysis of unsolicited comments.

References

Association of American Colleges. Liberal Learning and the Arts and Sciences Major. Vol. 1: The Challenge of Connecting Learning. Washington, D.C.: Association of American Colleges, 1991a.
Association of American Colleges. Liberal Learning and the Arts and Sciences Major. Vol. 2: Reports from the Fields. Washington, D.C.: Association of American Colleges, 1991b.
Becher, T. "Disciplinary Discourse." Studies in Higher Education, 1987, 12, 261–274.
Becher, T. Academic Tribes and Territories: Intellectual Enquiry and the Cultures of Disciplines. Bristol, Penn.: Society for Research into Higher Education and Open University Press, 1989.

Biglan, A. "The Characteristics of Subject Matter in Different Scientific Areas." *Journal of Applied Psychology*, 1973a, *57*, 195–203.

Biglan, A. "Relationships Between Subject Matter Characteristics and the Structure and Output of University Departments." *Journal of Applied Psychology*, 1973b, *57*, 204–213.

Donald, J. G. "Knowledge Structures: Methods for Exploring Course Content." *Journal of Higher Education*, 1983, *54*, 31–41.

Donald, J. G. "University Professors' Views of Knowledge and Validation Processes." *Journal of Educational Psychology*, 1990, *82*, 242–249.

Donald, J. G. "The Development of Thinking Processes in Postsecondary Education: Application of a Working Model." *Higher Education*, 1992, *24*, 413–430.

Dressel, P. L., and Marcus, D. *On Teaching and Learning in College: Reemphasizing the Roles of Learners and the Disciplines in Liberal Education.* San Francisco: Jossey-Bass, 1982.

Kolb, D. A. "Management and the Learning Processes." *California Management Review*, 1976, *18*, 21–31.

Kolb, D. A. "Learning Styles and Disciplinary Differences." In A. W. Chickering and Associates, *The Modern American College: Responding to the New Realities of Diverse Students and a Changing Society.* San Francisco: Jossey-Bass, 1981.

Kuhn, T. S. *The Structure of Scientific Revolutions.* (2nd ed., enlarged) Chicago: University of Chicago Press, 1970.

Lattuca, L. R., and Stark, J. S. "Modifying the Major: Extemporaneous Thoughts from Ten Disciplines." Paper presented at the 18th annual meeting of the Association for the Study of Higher Education, Pittsburgh, Penn., Nov. 4–7, 1993.

Lattuca, L. R., and Stark, J. S. "Will Disciplinary Perspectives Impede Curricular Reform?" *Journal of Higher Education*, in press.

Lodahl, J. B., and Gordon, G. "The Structure of Scientific Fields and the Functioning of University Graduate Departments." *American Sociological Review*, 1972, *37*, 57–72.

Phenix, P. H. *Realms of Meaning: A Philosophy of the Curriculum for General Education.* New York: McGraw-Hill, 1986.

Stark, J. S., Lowther, M. A., Bentley, R. J., Ryan, M. P., Martens, G. G., Genthon, M. L., Wren, P., and Shaw, K. M. *Planning Introductory College Courses: Influences of Faculty.* Ann Arbor, Mich.: NCRIPTAL, 1990.

Stark, J. S., Lowther, M. A., Ryan, M. P., Bomotti, S. S., Genthon, M. L., Haven, C. L., and Martens, G. G. *Reflections on Course Planning: Faculty and Students Consider Influences and Goals.* Ann Arbor, Mich.: NCRIPTAL, 1988.

Toulmin, S. E. *Human Understanding.* Vol. 1. Princeton, N.J.: Princeton University Press, 1972.

JOAN S. STARK is professor of higher education, University of Michigan.

LISA R. LATTUCA is a doctoral candidate at the University of Michigan.

PART THREE

The Major as a Teaching and
Learning Community

Examining the language used to describe the liberal arts major leads to new insights. We may find the keys to reform lurking among the hidden metaphors.

Unlocking the Doors: From Separate to Connected Knowing

Elaine P. Maimon

In educational reform, as in everything else, the doors of perception are constructed of language. The words we use to describe experience define our vistas. If we are to see undergraduate education and liberal arts majors in a new way, we must closely examine the language we conventionally use about that education. What can we learn from the hidden metaphors in the everyday language of education? Is it possible that the very words we use to describe undergraduate education can block our efforts to rethink what we do? This chapter explores the language that we use to talk about the academic major. The goal is reform, that is, renewal, through our seeing forms, images, and, most importantly, words in new ways. Interrogating our metaphors can bring about change. By looking at language, we can unlock the doors of perception.

The word *major* itself implies comparative size and importance, thereby emphasizing a quantification of credits and hours. It is a comparative term in a hierarchical structure. If the major is more, then something else is less. Implicit in the idea of the major is that a major is the most significant subset of a concrete whole, a portion or chunk of something with defined boundaries. The word major thus works at cross-purposes to the concept of the curriculum as a living intellectual community.

Limits of Specialization

We are also talking quantitatively when we refer to someone's academic specialization. As used in biology, specialization means adaptation to a specific environment in order to survive. We say that a species achieves specialization. In the academy, *specialization* is what students think they want when they ask

NEW DIRECTIONS FOR HIGHER EDUCATION, no. 84, Winter 1993 © Jossey-Bass Publishers

for career preparation. Students too often want to complete distribution requirements as quickly and conveniently as possible and then get down to majoring in a field that sounds the same as the name of a job: accounting, prelaw, premedicine, predentistry. One reason students avoid majoring in philosophy is that they do not think they can make a living as philosophers. In higher education, we too often develop curricula to appeal to students' desire for mere specialization. We train our captive charges in the skills they erroneously believe will enable them to survive in a specific environment or occupation. Rather than reinforcing their narrow ideas, we should develop curricula that challenge students' initial assumptions about the knowledge that will best prepare them for living and working in the world.

The student population at Queens College, where I teach, is more inclined than most college populations to seek narrowly defined technical specializations leading toward readily identifiable jobs—usually jobs that the students have already encountered: doctor, lawyer, accountant, teacher. These narrow goals are at odds with the fifty-year mission of Queens College, one of the four original liberal arts colleges (along with Hunter, City, and Brooklyn Colleges) in the City University of New York. From the time of its founding, Queens College has served as a bridge over which a first-generation immigrant population moves from the neighborhood boundaries to a wider world. The immigrants and children of immigrants who attend Queens College have publicly funded opportunities to move from a literal-minded view about what it means to be educated to a more sophisticated understanding of liberal learning. Indeed, Queens College is sometimes called Ellis Island University. Sixty-six native languages are spoken in its classrooms. But the current generation of Queens College students, reflecting the accelerating fragmentation and anomie of the city itself, seems rigidly committed to narrow definitions of competence, even as profound changes in the nature and organization of work make broader definitions essential. As Richard Lanham points out (1990), immigrant groups earlier in this century came from successive countries in waves and sought assimilation into an agrarian and then industrial society. Today's immigrants come from dozens of cultures and languages all at once and no longer enter an industrial society that rewards willing hands. At the beginning of the twentieth century, work—and overwork—could always be found in factories and sweatshops; children would leave school far too early because their hands were needed to support the family. We know the abuses and losses of that age, but we sometimes forget that the industrial society placed a lesser burden on education because even the uneducated could support themselves with willing hands.

Essential Learning

The responsibility of education is far greater today when the industrial society has been replaced by an information society. The vast majority of jobs today involve the exchange of information or the performance of a service. Willing hands are no longer rewarded. Even if we see some needed recovery in this nation's manufacturing base, we will never return to a time when high motivation and skill in a mechanical craft can compensate for the absence of a broad education. Several generations ago, a trained toolmaker could support himself for a lifetime with his specialty, but specialization is no longer a mode of economic survival. When plants close, even the best toolmakers are laid off. An information society rewards linguistic and numerical competence. In simple terms, students must read, write, speak, and count, if they are simply to survive economically in the twenty-first century. If they are to thrive, they must also question everything they read, write, speak, or count. Literacy, numeracy, and critical thinking are the responsibilities of everyone involved in education everywhere and at every level. Communication, defined broadly, is the essential skill needed by the diverse Queens College student body. And as various demographic studies make clear, as Queens College is today, so many college and universities will be, sooner rather than later.

Toward a New Understanding of Expertise

College students, whether their first language is English or Hindi, must understand how to use complex symbol systems in a variety of situations. Words, numbers, and pictures must become the natural parlance for all students. Such skill in communication cannot be inculcated without a full-scale effort from the entire higher education community. The task cannot be assigned to freshman English or to a series of distribution requirements. We must find means to help students transcend specialization in order to be prepared for the new world. Competence with complex symbol systems means understanding the various languages used within academic and nonacademic communities. Although students may falsely assume that academic disciplines are defined by different sets of facts, we know that disciplines are actually distinguished by forms of representation and ways of asking questions. A physicist represents the phenomenon of a wave by a numerical formula that allows us to ask questions about sounds on the radio and about the tides of the sea. A poet represents radios and oceans in very different ways. Without our help, students adopt an undifferentiated approach to academic study. Physics and poetry alike can seem boring to students when viewed from a monolithic perspective. Students literally cannot see what is supposed to be so interesting. If students are helped to perceive the differing symbol systems taken for granted in the academy, they will be better prepared to identify the various languages used in the worlds beyond the campus. The legal community reads a Supreme Court decision—Planned Parenthood of Southeastern Pennsylvania v. Casey, for example—in terms of Constitutional tests: "strict scrutiny" as opposed to "undue burden." Politicians read the same decision in terms of constituencies and coalitions: conservatives, moderates, and liberals; pro-choice, pro-life. If students are unprepared to recognize subtle shifts in the terms used in specialized conversation, they will lose confidence in their ability to move within and among the complex worlds where the ground is forever shifting. If we can assist students in gaining competence in various forms of translation, then and only then will they find a voice in many different conversations.

An emphasis on linguistic competence brings us to another metaphor used for the academic major, that of *expertise*. The student who majors in a discipline begins as a novice and then, through the guidance of mature practitioners, approaches a degree of expertise—one that can be exemplified in the language of a senior thesis or project, for example. Etymologically, at least, expertise works better than specialization as a modern metaphor for major. *Expertise,* with its Latin root *experiri* (to try), connotes ongoing experimentation. A specialist becomes adapted to a specific environment; an expert, in this etymological sense of explorer, continues to try new things. The word *expert* also denotes the highest grade that can be achieved in marksmanship, describing the ability to see and hit the target throughout several trials.

Cultivating Peripheral Vision. The hidden metaphors in the word *expertise* imply that teachers educate students to try and, then, through the teachers' mentoring, to see clearly within a changing landscape. Other words with embedded metaphors of sight are also useful in discussing the major. *Integrity in the College Curriculum: A Report to the Academic Community* (Association of American Colleges, 1985) argues that "focused study" should convey to the student a sense of "both the possibilities and limits of such study." What that means is that we must help students not merely to focus but also to cultivate peripheral vision. A student who merely focuses will often miss the subtle interchanges between figure and ground.

The paintings of Jasper Johns make use of the classic figure-ground images that beginning psychology students study in their chapters on perception: the old woman who viewed again becomes the young woman, the vase that looked at differently becomes two faces in profile. Johns's work reminds us that a single focus may not be sufficient to comprehend the postmodern world. Nick Carraway, the narrator of *The Great Gatsby,* says that perhaps the world is best viewed through a single window. Nick himself focuses on the story of Jay Gatsby as a way of understanding the world of the 1920s (Fitzgerald, [1925] 1953). Jasper Johns may be saying that the world of the 1990s must be viewed through many windows. Focus, but know how to *re*focus. Imagine and *re*imagine. Form and *re*form. Live with paradox and complexity. Be aware of the center and of the periphery. Peripheral vision is also the subject of Michelangelo Antonioni's film *Blow-Up.* The photographer in *Blow-Up* misses the second appearance of the murderer because he is focused on his lovemaking with the two teenage groupies who have come to his studio. As the photographer rolls around on sheets of large white photographic paper, the audience also focuses on the salacious scene in the center and misses the moment of truth when the mysterious stranger appears off to the side. The solution to the puzzle will often appear on the periphery. Similarly, focused study and expertise may open the doors straight ahead while those on the side remain closed. And who knows who may be waiting to enter from the wings?

James Voss, professor of psychology at the University of Pittsburgh, in his study of the differing behavior of experts and novices, places an important emphasis on the kind of vision that sees the periphery as well as the center (Voss, 1989). He points to the physics expert who works out a problem by spending a relatively large amount of time representing the problem, often by drawing a diagram or by another visual means. The representation allows the expert to discern the category into which a particular problem fits. Once the expert sees the characteristics of the problem at hand, she or he can match those characteristics to the pattern of a class of similar problems stored in memory. Experts regularly go through this process of representing patterns and connections. Novices almost never do.

Connected knowing, focusing, and refocusing, all these ideas encompassed in the etymology of expertise challenge faculty's traditional compulsion toward *coverage*. As *The Challenge of Connecting Learning* (Association of American Colleges, 1991), points out, "the problem with the major is not that it has failed to deliver certain kinds of knowledge. The problem is that it often delivers too much knowledge with too little attention to how that knowledge is being created, what methods and modes of inquiry are employed in its creation, what presuppositions inform it, and what entailments flow from its particular ways of knowing" (p. 6). In other words, we can cover only that which remains static. But what are we covering *up* in our frenzy to cover the world? And should we not, as Donald McQuade of U.C. Berkeley's English department asks, be *uncovering* material instead of covering it?

Expertise Versus Authority. The expert in Voss's sense is an experimenter, uncovering new material and new directions, searching for ever-changing patterns, denying stasis. This expert makes connections in a dynamic world. But this exploratory sense of expertise is rarely communicated in common parlance. Today, the etymology of expertise is hardly visible under layers of connotation, and too often expertise is used as a synonym for *authority*, a word that gets in the way of reform. Authority is a hierarchical term that implies the power to enforce laws, exact obedience, determine, or judge. Authority implies the closing off of peripheral vision, since authoritative statements posit certainty, not possibility. Christopher Cerf's hilarious book *The Experts Speak: The Definitive Compendium of Authoritative Misinformation* (1984) illustrates expertise corrupted into authority at the same time as it shows how often the voice of authority is wrong. Here for example, is a pronouncement from an authority in economics, Yale professor Irving Fisher, writing on October 17, 1929: "Stocks have reached what looks like a permanently high plateau." I wish Cerf would write a sequel to deflate the all-too-recent analyses by political scientists, the State Department, the Pentagon, and the CIA on U.S.-Soviet relations in the days of the "Evil Empire." As Richard J. Barnet comments, "There are file drawers of contingency plans in the Pentagon for fighting all kinds of wars that can never be fought, but the White House clearly had no contingency plans for what to do in case of Cold War victory" (1990, p. 66). After that small oversight, the same authorities a brief time later made definitive pronouncements denying the very possibility of the Soviet Union becoming, in short order, the former Soviet Union. We cannot fault specialists on the former Soviet Union because they did not make accurate predictions. Vision does not have to imply second sight. Yet experts in the 1990s have had many dramatic lessons on the importance of peripheral vision. Perhaps we need a new kind of higher education to avoid the mistakes of the past, to teach students to question authority, especially their own, and to open their eyes to multiple possibilities.

Some of the most significant books on specific social topics published in the latter half of the twentieth century were not written by authorities but by *amateurs,* that is, people who engage in a science or art for love, not money. In a recent article in *The New York Times Book Review,* Robert Fulford (1992) points to *The Death and Life of Great American Cities* as "the most influential single work in the history of town planning," one that "simultaneously helped to kill off the modern movement in architecture." The author, Jane Jacobs, was neither a town planner nor an architect; she was a magazine editor. Fulford points to other examples: Paul Goodman's *Growing Up Absurd* (1960), which "tackled the specialized subject of youth and delinquency in a way that was startlingly fresh" (Fulford, 1992); Rachel Carson's *Silent Spring* (1962), a seminal book in the environmental movement, written by a person with an M.A. in marine biology; Betty Friedan's *The Feminine Mystique* (1963), which created the second wave of twentieth-century feminism; Marshall McLuhan's *Understanding Media;* and Ralph Nader's *Unsafe at Any Speed.* One book that Fulford does not mention is Michael Harrington's *The Other America* (1961), which inspired the Kennedy-Johnson war on poverty. At the time of writing the book, Harrington held an M.A. in English literature. Nonetheless, Queens College hired him as a full professor of political science. All these amateurs were people with expertise in the sense of hitting the mark. They also had peripheral vision. We could have no better goal for those who major in our disciplines than that they become amateurs, lovers of learning, unrestrained in their vision by the artificial barriers set up by specialists.

Paradoxically, the preparation of undergraduates who intend to go on to graduate school might best be viewed as the preparation of amateurs, in the etymological sense of people with passionate commitment. Graduate students, who are expected eventually to contribute to the knowledge in a field, must have the capacity for vision and revision. Even more importantly, graduate students should feel the amateur's love for the work—the sustaining passion that transforms the pain of growing into a joy.

Crossing Borders, Connecting Communities

Joseph William of the University of Chicago reminds us that we cannot graph growth toward expertise in the linear way that we measure height or weight.

Expertise may not be a step-by-step progression to some unseen nirvana but instead a process of connecting oneself with a community—although *not* a single, narrowly defined community of specialists. An expert has mastered the process of moving from one specialized circle to another, from one context, one community, to another. The expert, as opposed to the specialist, can tolerate the frustration of learning something new. The specialist lives in a closed, secure inner circle. The expert moves from context to context, unafraid of initially appearing clumsy. The expert moves undaunted into new territory. The specialist is embarrassed by mistakes; the expert learns from mistakes and grows. The expert feels sufficiently at home in one area of study that she or he can move comfortably into new areas. In their article "Transforming Scholarship," David Scott and Susan Awbrey (1993, p. 39) envision a "Connected University." They quote Benjamin Barber, who captures the essential paradox of expertise: "The great artists, scientists, and paradigm shifters, in their apprenticeship, first became well versed in the genres whose boundaries they later explored" (p. 39). In the undergraduate major as in life in general, those who really feel at home in one place have enough confidence to travel.

The Challenge of Connecting Learning (Association of American Colleges, 1991) gives particular attention to the metaphor of the academic major as a *home.* I find that metaphor the most useful of all. It is certainly preferable to specialization, as I have just explained that term. As a metaphor, *home* is also preferable to the term *study in depth.* If we picture students ferreting deeper and deeper into the earth, as they become more advanced in subject matter, then we must also picture them striving against knowledge, against a resistant element. My own mental image for study in depth is not digging in the unyielding, positivist earth but, instead, plumbing the depths of yielding water. My preferred image is probably connected to an inspiring speech I heard in 1975—a speech that changed my life. At a meeting of the Modern Language Association, Mina Shaughnessy of the City University of New York called upon the assembled faculty to stop resisting the new populations of students who were entering the university under its open admissions policy. She asked us to pass through several developmental phases—"guarding the gates" and "converting the natives"—to the highest form of development, which she called "diving in," meaning that we should leave the comfortable shores of old educational assumptions and dive into the new challenges posed by new generations of students. We should immerse ourselves with our students in the changing tides of knowledge.

Majors as Homes for Liberal Learning

Still, study in depth, even in yielding water, may sometimes connote being at sea or even drowning. So, of all the metaphors used for the major, home is the one that works best. I do not expect, however, that the first item on educators' agenda should be to change the word *major* to *home.* Such an *Architectural*

Digest approach to curriculum change would certainly be a misallocation of much-needed energy. Yet some institutions have dropped the word major from their catalogues. Brown University, for example, uses the term concentration. Although concentration can carry some unwelcome connotations of density and of focus without peripheral vision, concentration has its etymological root in the center, a coming together toward a common center (Latin con centrum), a community, a home.

The Challenge of Connecting Learning draws upon the idea of community when it cites John Higham's description of the contemporary academy as a "house in which the inhabitants are leaning out of the many open windows gaily chatting with the neighbors, while the doors between the rooms stay closed" (Association of American Colleges, 1991, p. 15). As the title of this chapter suggests, I am in favor of unlocking the doors. What does that mean? First of all, let me distinguish between houses and homes. A house is a structure built on a foundation. A home, in contrast, can exist without a definable physical structure, as when we say we "feel at home." Home is a feeling— social, psychological, spiritual—of security, happiness, refuge, and care. A house is built according to a blueprint, something that must be followed in precise detail, but faculty members will not teach from blueprints, and students cannot become liberally educated by learning algorithms. Academic majors cannot be houses. In contrast to the blueprints from which a house is built, a home has a *matrix*. Matrix comes from the Latin word *mater* (mother), and its first meaning is "womb." Living organisms emerge from matrices. Living academic majors emerge from guidelines, not blueprints. The matrix, with its gendered association of women and homes, also implies dialogue, negotiation, connection.

In John Higham's view, the contemporary academy is a house, a physical structure, with many rooms, or departments, which are homes to their scholarly inhabitants. Today, Higham suggests, the faculty who live in these departments are engaged in lively cross-disciplinary exchanges; that is why they are "leaning out of the many open windows gaily chatting with the neighbors." Open windows are all to the good since they bring in fresh air from the world outside. But it does seem inefficient to keep the doors between the rooms locked. If the doors were open, at least once in a while, the cross-circulation of ideas would be even livelier. I am not suggesting that we knock down the walls or remove the doors from their hinges or even keep the doors perpetually open. I am suggesting only that we unlock the doors between the rooms. And if we visualize the front door as the point of access for students, then the removal of locks must extend to that crucial front gateway, which students should be able to enter without first being issued keys. Once students enter the academic house, they should find common spaces, curricular and co-curricular, where they can converse cordially with each other and with faculty. These common spaces are important not just for newcomers to the house but also for residents of the upper floors, those we have conventionally called upperclassmen. In other words, we should find ways to involve students at all stages of instruction and faculty at all levels of seniority in general interest courses, in clubs, and in simply breaking bread together. Jonathan Smith has spoken of "creating social space without residency" as our biggest challenge today in higher education (Smith, 1992).

At Queens College, an urban commuter college of 18,000, where the centrifugal forces drawing everyone away from the center are stronger than any others I have ever experienced, educators and administrators have to exert special energies toward creating these communal spaces in the academic house. Left to their own devices, students and faculty would spend as little time on campus as possible. Nearly all the students have jobs off campus. Nearly all the professors would rather be in Manhattan than in Queens. Students choose their courses by the times they are offered. Those students who do stay on campus long enough to ask a question after class are too often confronted by professors who answer impatiently, giving the impression that any delay will make them late for an appearance on the "MacNeil/Lehrer News Hour." The college has to devote conscious, herculean efforts to creating a home for students and faculty in Queens. Among these efforts are opportunities for faculty to work in a mentoring relationship with students. Students can, for example, compete for opportunities to work as undergraduate research assistants for faculty. Under these circumstances, students can find intellectual employment on campus rather than willing-hands employment at McDonald's. The relationship with the faculty member becomes one of partnership. The student is now helping with the research that the faculty member will later present at a symposium or in a scholarly paper coauthored with the undergraduate or even on the "MacNeil/Lehrer News Hour." Several departments have used scarce resources to set up computer lounges specifically for their undergraduate students. At first, perhaps, students come to these communal spaces because they offer special rights to equipment that the students would have to wait in line for at the computer center. But once in the lounge, students talk and work with other students in the department and with faculty. At Queens, academic clubs take on special importance. Poetry readings organized by the English club, a speaker invited by the anthropology club, or a field trip organized by the geology club quite literally create special spaces in which students can feel at home. We have also developed the concept of the honors minor in business and in journalism. Students who qualify for these minors have their own computer-equipped communal space within the Queens academic house. And our computer lounge also has a television set.

I want, at least, to state my plea that colleges teach visual literacy and critical thinking about television in all parts of the curriculum. For the last twenty-five years, owing to snobbery or Luddism, we have left students to their own devices vis à vis television. Just as parents should watch television with their children in order to discuss what they see, educators should be using television as a text. If they do not, then they will condemn another generation to the tyranny of the sound bite. However, further discussion of this subject and ideas for bringing television into the academic home will have to be the subject matter for another essay.

The academic house becomes a home also through hospitality, the preparation for and celebration with visitors. In the honors minor at Queens, the college creates opportunities for students to interact with interesting people from outside the academy. Guests from the corporate and journalism advisory boards visit with undergraduate students, provide internships, and then, after graduation, open opportunities in the world outside the academic home. Through these special programs, it is at least possible for the Queens College student to find a room that feels like her or his own. If students are lucky, they will find a department that has a mentoring program, student clubs, a computer lounge, a television, and a videocassette recorder. Or they will join the business or journalism minor, where faculty members and more experienced students are making efforts to help them feel at home. If they are very lucky indeed, they will find faculty who are not hanging out the windows of the house, with their backs toward the students, but are instead walking freely through the doors between the rooms. If students find faculty who understand how to make connections, then they have a chance to develop capacities for connected knowing. If students find faculty who understand that people and fields of study can make connections with others without losing their own identity, then those students will be confident enough in their expertise in a particular discipline to talk with others who have been asking different questions and reading different books. Students will share their thinking and finally test the boundaries of their expertise. Only those who do not feel at home with themselves fear absorption by others. Those who feel at home in the connected university will have the confidence to travel.

Unlocking the Doors

After being transported by the pages of this volume to the realms of the ideal major, we, too, must return home to our campuses to do some remodeling or, at least, some thorough housecleaning. Let me offer some recommendations.

On every campus we find a certain number of colleagues who will never change. Every academic house has its agoraphobics—those who are so insecure about the world outside that they want every detail of the home environment to remain inviolable. The only students these agoraphobics consider worth teaching are those who appear to be younger clones of the agoraphobics themselves. All others are admissions office mistakes. We cannot waste energy trying to change these agoraphobics even if we are dismayed by them. Not even the most excellent curriculum committee report will substitute for the real need here—years of analysis. Fortunately, agoraphobics are not the majority on any campus, even if they sometimes seem to be. Nor are the change agents the majority on any campus. Change is difficult. Change hurts. But I am convinced of two basic principles that can bring about positive change. First, most of our colleagues would rather do a good job than a bad job, and second, nearly every faculty member *wants something*. We must find out what each faculty member wants and use that as an incentive for change. Sometimes what is wanted is as simple as recognition for changes already made. From the perspective of organizational behavior, what we must find is the intersection between the needs of the individual and the needs of the institution.

Once we have gathered a willing group of faculty members, we can unlock the doors for students. We can develop mentoring opportunities on campus, including research partnerships between faculty members and undergraduates. We can consciously create spaces for students to live in as their intellectual homes, with computers, comfortable chairs, televisions, music, and food. We can build connections between the rooms of our academic houses through research institutes, cross-disciplinary study, and writing across the curriculum, and we can map out possible routes for students to follow from room to room and also to the common spaces. We can explicitly teach students to be colleagues by helping them to organize study groups and by modeling for them our own intellectual lives as scholars, teachers, writers, and colleagues. We can develop programs for student–faculty research, peer tutors, and undergraduate writing associates. We can find ways, even in apocalyptic times for budgets, to offer enough small classes so that every student has at least one opportunity each semester to be more than a face in the crowd. We can organize programs that invite visitors from the world of business, journalism, government, and social service to interact with students. I am talking about more than just the guest lecture. I mean advisory boards that take an active role in reviewing departmental curricula and making suggestions from outside the academic house.

Most importantly, we can develop institutional policies that allow us to keep and to honor those who make the academic house into a home. Right now, for the most part, we reward those who keep their backs to the door and lean over their own specialized work. We must expand our definition of publication beyond the confines of narrowly defined disciplinary journals. Otherwise, we will perpetuate the idea that the only ones who deserve tenure and promotion are the mere specialists among us. We must find ways to reward serious intellectual work, even when it serves the public good. In other words, we must reward faculty who "go public" with their ideas in general interest magazines and newspapers, public lectures, and consultations with schools and businesses. And, of course, we must find systematic, nonsentimental ways to assess and reward teaching. The teaching portfolios developed by the American Association of Higher Education are promising developments. If we can set up committees to assess scholarly publication, we can set up committees to review syllabi and course assignments in terms of their intellectual content. We can also ask candidates for tenure to explain their educational philosophy and goals and to place course materials and student tasks within that intellectual context. Such procedures would encourage faculty to regard teaching with the same seriousness now reserved only for scholarship.

We can find new forms and new language for what we do. In fact, we must. What we do in the academy is more important than we may realize. In our relatively protected environment, we can set an example for rethinking boundaries and homelands. Do we choose balkanization or community? Perhaps the connected university will illuminate the way for a new generation of world citizens. Unlocking the doors to new ways of seeing, speaking, and learning will allow students and instructors to create vibrant connections with each other and with the wider world.

References

Association of American Colleges. *Integrity in the College Curriculum: A Report to the Academic Community*. Washington, D.C.: Association of American Colleges, 1985.

Association of American Colleges. *Liberal Learning and the Arts and Sciences Major*. Vol. 1: *The Challenge of Connecting Learning*. Washington, D.C.: Association of American Colleges, 1991.

Barnet, R. J. "Reflections: After the Cold War." *The New Yorker*, 1990, 65 (46), 65–76.

Cerf, C. *The Experts Speak: The Definitive Compendium of Authoritative Misinformation*. New York: Pantheon Books, 1984.

Fitzgerald, F. S. *The Great Gatsby*. New York: Charles Scribner's Sons, 1953. (Originally published 1925.)

Fulford, R. "When Jane Jacobs Took on the World." *The New York Times Book Review*, Feb. 16, 1992, pp. 3, 28–29.

Lanham, R. "The Extraordinary Convergence: Democracy, Technology, Theory, and the University Curriculum." *South Atlantic Quarterly*, 1990, 89 (1), 27–49.

Scott, D. A., and Awbrey, S. M. "Transforming Scholarship." *Change*, July/Aug. 1993, pp. 38–43.

Smith, J. "What Students Should Expect from a Major." Paper presented at the Association of American Colleges Conference on Re-Forming the Major, Philadelphia, Feb. 20–23, 1992.

Voss, J. "On the Composition of Experts and Novices." In E. Maimon and F. W. O'Connor, *Thinking, Reasoning, and Writing*. White Plains, N.Y.: Longman, 1989.

ELAINE P. MAIMON is dean of experimental programs and professor of English at Queens College, City University of New York.

To place the major in the center of liberal education calls for faculty to reshape academic departments as teaching and learning collectives that adapt the practices of disciplinary professionalism for education purposes.

The Disciplines of Liberal Learning

William Scott Green

To advocate the disciplinary major as the core of liberal education is to flout the conventional wisdom about what is wrong with college learning in the United States. In the view of contemporary critics, the intellectual specialization represented by disciplinary study is the source of higher education's shortcomings-the academy's equivalent of original sin. Critics complain that U.S. college curricula have become diffuse and aimless, that colleges lack a sense of community, and that professors teach neglectfully and too little (Kimball, 1989). They blame scholarly specialization for the disciplinary loyalties, cloistered departmentalism, and fragmented curricula that allegedly rob college learning of shared goals, values, and meaning. They charge that specialized knowledge creates a culture of limited expertise, which artificially constricts the curriculum, suppresses diversity and alternate ways of knowing, and produces authoritarian and impersonal teaching. The critique of specialization carries with it a deep suspicion of faculty professionalization, particularly as it is manifest in the culture, and perhaps the practice, of research. In 1985, the Association of American Colleges' report *Integrity in the College Curriculum* summed up all these concerns most succinctly: "the development that overwhelmed the old curriculum and changed the entire nature of higher education was the transformation of the professors from teachers concerned with the characters and minds of their students to professionals, scholars with Ph.D. degrees with an allegiance to academic disciplines stronger than their commitment to teaching or to the life of the institutions where they are employed" (p. 6).

Note: I am grateful to Deborah Derylak, who helped enormously with the research for this article, and to my colleagues Celia Applegate, Dale McAdam, Suzanne O'Brien, and Richard Aslin for constructive critical readings.

On the grounds that specialization is the root of our educational ills, many reform proposals in the 1980s advanced structured core curricula or programs of general education as primary ways to integrate undergraduate learning and thereby develop and nurture community. For example, Lynne V. Cheney's 50 Hours: A Core Curriculum for College Students (1989) recommended a required program of sixteen semester courses, extending through the junior year, with the claim that, among other benefits, a required core brings "needed order and coherence" to undergraduate learning (p. 2) and "provides a context for forming the parts of education into a whole" (p. 12). Likewise, Ernest Boyer's College: The Undergraduate Experience in America (1987) advocated an "integrated core," extending over four years, to give students "a more integrated view of knowledge and a more authentic view of life" by overcoming "the fragmentation and specialization of the academy" (pp. 90–91).

This volume takes a different approach to the problem of liberal education at the turn of the millennium. Instead of starting from the perspective of time-honored and evocative curricular memories, it addresses what its contributors judge to be the realities of the academic present. Since World War II, academic disciplines have become "the principal, even exclusive way, to organize legitimate curricula and faculty professional work" (Weaver, 1991, p. 25). Whether we like it or not, the professional mission of most contemporary faculty members is shaped largely by a field of knowledge, an area of study. Whether we like it or not, disciplinary professionalism, more than any other factor, fixes the divisions within contemporary college curricula, programs, and courses. To be sure, the professoriate created these conditions and could move to change them. But such pervasive undoing of the world's most ambitious and successful system of higher learning seems unlikely, surely for the near term. Instead of trying to dismantle the foundations of the faculty's professionalism, this volume asks what will happen if we build on them. Instead of devising programs that countervail against intellectual specialization, it explores if, and how, the college faculty's disciplinary professionalism can become a vehicle to achieve educational goals traditionally associated with liberal learning. Hence, instead of addressing the curriculum in general, this volume focuses on the learning in particular that distinguishes college from high school, the concentrated study in and of a field of knowledge, the major.

What would it mean to make the major into a primary, perhaps the primary, path to a liberal education? At least three basic changes in the accepted practice and purpose of college study would result. First, placing the major at the center of liberal education calls into question the established categories of general and specialized learning in college study. Second, a focus on the major shifts the center of curricular and educational change from the college to the department. Finally, from the standpoint of the major, the mark of liberal education is less the study of many subjects than an attitude about learning, a resourcefulness grounded in awareness of where knowledge comes from and how it is made. These themes inform the arguments that follow.

Why General Education Isn't

The move to reconceive the major rather than to rejuvenate (yet again!) general education is not merely a concession to the faculty's disciplinary professionalism. Rather, general education, as conventionally understood, can neither theoretically nor practically address the problems of intellectual fragmentation, the lack of community, and neglectful teaching that critics think afflict U.S. higher education. There are reasons why general studies cannot make college learning whole.

To begin, consider how disparate from one another the fields of learning really are. A review (see Chapter One) of Stephen Toulmin's nearly classic theoretical description of "the variety of rational enterprises," which covers most of the fields and subjects typically taught and studied in college, makes the divisions plain (1972, pp. 359–411). Toulmin explains that a "rationally developing 'discipline'" emerges when a "shared commitment to a sufficiently agreed set of ideas leads to the development of an isolable and self-defining repertory of procedures; and where those procedures are open to further modification, so as to deal with problems arising from the incomplete fulfillment of those disciplinary ideals." Toulmin trenchantly distinguishes among "compact disciplines," "diffuse disciplines," "would-be disciplines," and "non-disciplinary activities." Compact disciplines, such as atomic physics, are methodologically and institutionally coherent. They exhibit a high level of agreement about collective ideals, procedures, modes of argument, and criteria of adequacy, and they have efficient professional meetings and organizations. Subfields within compact disciplines are likely to be pragmatic and procedural, and specialized journals contain a "substantial amount of cross-citation." In contrast, diffuse and would-be disciplines, which include most of the social sciences and humanities, often are loosely organized professionally and lack "a clearly defined, generally agreed reservoir of disciplinary problems." These characteristics thwart consistent critical testing of new concepts and procedures. Diffuse and would-be disciplines may "even lack common standards for deciding what constitutes a genuine problem, a valid explanation, or sound theory." In these fields, Toulmin argues, theoretical debate is "largely . . . methodological or philosophical . . . directed less at interpreting particular empirical findings than at debating the general acceptability (or unacceptability) of rival approaches, patterns of explanation, and standards of judgment." Subdisciplines in these areas tend to be ideological, even sectarian, and cross-citation is relatively infrequent. In nondisciplinary activities, where Toulmin classifies such fields as fine arts and ethics, "the very questions at issue are liable to be more complex, changeable, or even personal, than in a normal discipline. As a result, both the ecological demands of the particular situation and the criteria for judging conceptual novelties will be that much the less well-defined, settled, or agreed."

The most common model of general education offers students experience in a number of fields across the disciplinary spectrum, but Toulmin's analysis shows why this approach is an unlikely vehicle for integrated learning. How could a wide and necessarily superficial sampling among disciplines so disparate in intellectual endeavor, requirements, and habits produce intellectual unity, especially at the beginning of a college education? Many institutions recently have addressed this difficulty by developing related core courses designed to generate an intellectual commonality by supplying students with a shared set of learned references. But such commonality, a faculty's considered but unavoidably arbitrary construction, hardly qualifies as integrated learning for the student. It builds on faculty expertise in discrete fields, on precisely what students do not know and cannot know from a small sample of courses. A general problem in such programs is that the discrete pieces do not connect with one another. More important, they rarely connect with programs of specialized study, the one thing the students come to know well. General education cannot supply comprehensive coherence to an entire college education. It can produce order, but not meaning.

Moreover, general education is only general with respect to some particular. The very meaning of general is relative. Prescribed general education programs typically are no less restrictive than are programs of study in discrete fields. They are just restrictive in different ways. A "great books" curriculum may seem general with respect to literature or history, but it also seems narrow and specialized with respect to physics or computer science. General education can be broadening in the best sense (captured by an alumna of the University of Rochester, where I teach, who wrote, "That poetry course I had to take showed me a part of myself I didn't know was there"), but it also can be limiting and dulling (a current Rochester student complained, "I had to take a French course to satisfy my language requirement, and that made me put off an economics course that really interested me. I'm turned off to French for good!").

Even if general education does provide a common set of references for students and faculty—and only the most structured, and thus restrictive, programs do—it is a cumbersome vehicle for the development of community. Because general studies do not reflect the faculty's own graduate education, the institutional effort necessary to develop and maintain a general education program is disproportionate to the program's impact on students' learning. Often, faculty who work to develop or substantially revise general education requirements and programs are enervated by the process, and the task of sustaining the program over time falls to the administration, the campus unit least well equipped for it. A field of knowledge represents a cluster of problems, a set of data, and a heritage of curiosity that can form a discourse and define a community of inquiry. General education cannot constitute an area of knowledge because it was invented as an antidote to specialized study—that is, general education is cast only in terms of what it is not. As conventionally practiced, general education can provide students essential, valuable, and enriching exposure to unfamiliar fields and methods, and it can lead students to subjects they otherwise might have bypassed, but it can neither anchor a curriculum nor secure its overall coherence. Our preoccupation with general education has distracted us from the real foundation of undergraduate study, the major.

From College to Department

The limitations of general education as a solution to the problems of fragmentation and diminished community justify a new look at departments as centers of learning. The conception of the major as participation in a knowledge community and its discourse forces fresh attention on the faculty groups that constitute the actual community and shape the concrete discourse that students encounter.

Typically, though not always, academic departments reflect scholarly disciplines, and the purpose of disciplinary professionalism is to foster and facilitate research. Hence, a department's intellectual mission is likely to be shaped heavily, if not primarily, by its field's research agenda. If the major is to become a foundation of liberal education, the department's intellectual mission must be transformed into an educational one. But such a transformation requires understanding the department as more than a gathering of scholars and researchers and conceiving the major as more than a set of up-to-date courses. It means reinventing the department as a teaching and learning collective, in which the faculty, through collaboration with one another and with students, creates programs of study that draw students into learning both within and about a field of knowledge. If we are to use the major as a path to liberal learning, we need to realize the educational potential of disciplinary professionalism.

Hostility to disciplinary professionalism has obscured the contribution of specialized study to the goals of liberal education. An academic discipline forms the intellectual setting that nurtures a lifetime of learning, and it constitutes the forum in which new thinking is tested and assessed. Disciplines are loci of both criticism and self-criticism. They provide the context of public accountability for analysis, research, and interpretation, a framework of knowledge and thought essential for the crucial task of distinguishing insight from idiosyncrasy. Disciplines represent heritages of curiosity, and they are the concrete manifestations of shared interests. As they appear on discrete campuses in the form of departments, programs, committees, or the equivalent, the disciplines offer precisely the ingredients of intellectual community that college education in the United States is now widely believed to lack.

Disciplinary professionalism also is essential to good teaching. Many traits make for good college teaching, but primary among them is knowing something very well. The current preoccupation with enrollments and reten-tion—the consequence of severe market pressures—has led to a widespread confusion between instruction and student centeredness, between teaching well and paying attention to (and spending time with) undergraduates. These activities are not the same. The professoriate is more than a helping profession, and college teachers are not mere facilitators. Professing implies expertise. Only by knowing something very well can we convey to students its force and appeal. We cannot represent the power of the varied realms of inquiry and dis-course we want students to encounter unless we are deeply engaged with those realms ourselves. We cannot show them how knowledge is discovered, invented, constructed, and evaluated without laboring at it ourselves. In teach-ing, there is a small distance but a world of difference between critically pass-ing on the work of others, which is most of what we do in the classroom, and passing critical opinions about work we have not done and could not do. Only the former teaches respect for learning. Thus, even the ever-popular interdis-ciplinary studies assume disciplinary competence as their foundation. The scholarship required for effective teaching is discipline-based and therefore departmentally centered.

As a practical matter, reform of the college major depends on the ability of thousands of discrete academic departments to rethink the way they do business. Departmental cultures powerfully shape the aims and practice of teaching, and departmental curricula are far more capable than collegiate ones of reasonably rapid change. Too often administrators and faculty see depart-ments as bureaucratic or intellectual units rather than pedagogical ones. Too often, departments take corporate responsibility for everything but teaching. And too often, the result is insular and parochial learning that commits the errors the critics condemn. Disciplinary faculty members conceive themselves to inhabit a national or international realm of learning, a kind of intellectual heaven, in which disciplinary discourse and course content transcend cam-pus boundaries. For students, however, the campus is not a transient, earthly prelude to the sphere of celestial conversation. For students, the major is local. Committees of the guild—with scholarly input from around the globe—can devise learned curricula in their varied subjects, but the students' major com-prises eighteen to twenty-four months of partial, though fairly intense, study with a small number of teachers on a particular campus, and what students know of a field and how it works is a consequence of their experience with that group of teachers. To place the college major at the center of a liberal edu-cation shifts the focus of curricular change from the collegiate to the depart-mental faculty.

In U.S. higher education, academic departments are less than a century old, and their definition and institutional purpose are far from uniform. Departments vary in character and strength, even on a single campus, and their roles differ in disparate institutions. Some liberal arts colleges, particularly where departments are small, discourage departmental identity in favor of an institutional one. In research universities, where departments are the centers of graduate education, departmental boundaries tend to be high. The conventional university or college reward structure does not encourage the development of a corporate departmental ideology. When funds are short, administrations typically withdraw resources from the collective, that is, they cut departments and their budgets. Conversely, when resources are strong, administrations tend to disburse rewards to individuals, to the discrete faculty member. This sort of policy obscures departmental purpose. It discourages truly collective educational work and offers colleagues little reason to have a stake in one another's teaching. If departments are to be a center for curricular change, positive rewards will need to flow to departments as wholes rather than only to individual faculty members.

In principle, nothing about disciplinary teaching and learning obstructs the generalizing and critical perspective of liberal education. General learning is not learned generalization, and being able to generalize does not mean being a generalist. Thus, it is a common administrative wish, particularly for technical and scientific subjects, to assign introductory courses to the most senior and accomplished members of a field precisely because their deep understanding, achieved from within the discipline, allows them to generalize about and explain their field to beginners. Recent proposals for revising college learning implicitly equate the outlook of liberal learning with educational breadth. But critical perspective on knowledge requires more than peripheral vision, more than multiple outlooks. The self-consciousness about knowledge that truly distinguishes liberal education from both high school learning and technical training—the awareness, for instance, that knowledge is constructed, tentative, limited, and interpretive—is ineluctably a matter of depth. Meaningful and revealing perspective cannot be imposed on a field from without and is not achieved by adding yet another point of view. Rather, it emerges from within, from thinking one's way to the edge of a field, asking questions a discipline provokes but cannot answer, and moving outward to make connections. A generalizing perspective is grounded in experience and hard work in a field, not in an opinion about it. Liberal learning builds on the disciplines. It is not their antithesis.

Departmental Learning: Collectivity and Collaboration

Despite what critics have claimed, the current apparently poor fit between disciplinary professionalism and liberal learning does not result from overly limited subject matter or analytical focus. The issue is not specialization but narrowness: the intellectual selfishness that makes us disciplinary professionals poor and indifferent translators of what we know. To place the major at the center of liberal learning requires us to solve not a problem of restricted subject matter but a problem of restrictive and insular teaching. Despite our concern about maintaining fresh and contemporary course offerings, in our departments and our majors we keep too many of our interesting questions to ourselves. Within the major, students too infrequently are exposed to the reasons we, their teachers, find our fields compelling. We all too rarely share with students why our work is fun. In other words, we have not allowed our own disciplinary professionalism to serve as a model for education. We have not drawn our undergraduate majors in as colleagues so that they might, in ways appropriate for them, learn as we learn. Our failure to do this regularly and systematically in the liberal arts major is largely the consequence of the separation between research and teaching and our tendency to identify disciplinary professionalism only with research. This separation of research from teaching, which segregates the work faculty do with one another from work they do with their students, has roots deep in the history of higher education. The two institutional models from which U.S. higher education derives are the English college and the German research university. Although these institutions are very different in function and design, in both the work of learning is exam driven. In both, students' knowledge—their acquisition of education, so to speak—is certified by success on an examination. In both, teachers prepare students for tests only students will take, for work only students will do.

This division between the faculty's work and the students' work is the basis for the broadly held, but often unstated, conception of teaching as epiphenomenal rather than foundational. The separation undergirds the view of teaching as something distinct, even divergent, from research—of teaching as derivative intellectual work. Such a conception of teaching builds barriers between teachers and students. If teaching is secondary activity and something we do only to (or with) students, we will never be able to take students as seriously as we take ourselves, or their learning as seriously as our own. It is a short hop from secondary to second-rate. The sharp distinction between teaching and research carries with it a conception of the student as other, as someone whose intellectual life is somehow fundamentally different from, and fundamentally less than, our own.

One way to break the barrier between teaching and research, and the barrier between teacher and student that comes in its wake, is to reconceive the liberal arts major as a curriculum that employs the professional practices of a discipline to create a continuum of learning that draws students and faculty into one another's work. It is in the major that the heavenly realm of faculty discourse and the earthly arena of students' discovery should merge. A major conceived along these lines will help students develop a self-consciousness about how a field of learning works and will draw faculty into collective work that gives them a stake in one another's teaching.

Let me illustrate with a concrete example. In 1983, the administration of the College of Arts and Science at the University of Rochester transformed an interdepartmental program of religious studies into the Department of Religion and Classics. The department began its history with a dozen student majors. By 1993, that number had grown to over 120, in an undergraduate student body of fewer than 4,000. One reason for the department's success, in addition to good teaching, is that its programs of study are designed to encourage collective work among faculty, faculty and students, and students.

The department's major in religion requires ten courses: one introductory course in the Bible (Hebrew Bible or New Testament); one introductory course in the history of a religion (Judaism, Christianity, Islam, Religions of South Asia, or Religions of East Asia); one intermediate-level course in the nature of the field (Theories of Religion), required of all junior majors, with any course in religion as a prerequisite; six additional religion courses, no more than three of which can be in a single religion; and a senior seminar or senior tutorial in the field. The major has a structure, but not a rigid one. The introductory courses ensure that students have some capacity for critical use of the Bible, because of its importance in U.S. cultural and political life, and that they are familiar with the history and morphology of one major literate religion. The course in theories of religion supplies all religion majors with a common set of theoretical readings and a common frame of intellectual reference. The work of the senior year, whether as a seminar or a tutorial, draws upon and develops the work of the theories course.

Perhaps the most distinctive feature of the department's work is the way it systematically engages advanced majors in the education of beginning students. Junior and senior majors who did well in a required course (introductory and theories) work with (not for) the faculty in teaching that course. The theories course epitomizes this feature of the department's work. Typically, Theories of Religion has an enrollment of fifty to sixty students, most of them junior majors or minors in the department. The course is taught by a faculty member and two teaching fellows, senior majors who did well in the course in the previous year. The seniors receive academic credit, not money, for their work as fellows. The faculty member and the teaching fellows prepare the syllabus together and work collaboratively throughout the course.

The theories course requires roughly 200 pages of reading per week in primary scholarly works that have given the study of religion its disciplinary contours. The focus of the course is the quality of the argument in each work and the way each scholar conceives the subject of religion. Readings come from such fields as phenomenology, history of religion, psychology, anthropology, sociology, theology, and literary theory. Students are asked to explain how each writer distinguishes between religion and not-religion and how he or she defends that position. The theories course aims to help students understand that what appeared in some earlier course as a matter of fact about either religion in general or a particular religion actually depends on a theoretical argument, that is, on disciplined intellect and imagination. The course stresses the problem of generalization and asks students to use theoretical works to think about religion as an analytical category, to think about religion in general.

Each class is divided into three groups of approximately twenty students each, and each group meets with the teaching fellows, who work as a team, in a ninety-minute preparation section one or two days before the class meets as a whole. In these sections, students review the reading they will discuss later in the larger class, and they are required to bring with them a two-page restatement of the argument. The teaching fellows evaluate, but do not grade, these restatements and return them in the next class. The fellows also bring deficient restatements to the faculty member, who typically asks students having difficulties to rewrite their statements.

The work of the class itself consists of small-group presentations on the readings of the week. These presentations work as follows: Each week, a different team of two to four students presents a five- to ten-page critical analysis of the reading that the class has done. These teams review their analyses with the faculty member several days before the class meets as a whole, and they normally rewrite the paper twice before they present it. Thus, all students, even in a fairly large class, have the opportunity for small-group work with a faculty member. Students do most of the talking in the classes. Each class begins with presentation of the team's collective paper, which is distributed to all, and a discussion follows. Since all the students in principle (though not always in fact!) have previously read and discussed the reading, discussion usually moves at a fairly high level, and students have the chance to challenge one another's readings, interpretations, and thinking and to assess differences of opinion and judgment in a public forum with other knowledgeable readers. The teacher's role is to keep the discussion focused and to help bring conversation to closure. But, for the most part, the teacher sits on the sidelines, like a coach rather than a judge.

Although one faculty member is responsible for this course, all departmental faculty have either co-taught the course or taken it. The course varies slightly from year to year, but is built around a stable set of readings so it has continuity over time. It also is typical for departmental faculty members to drop in on the course for a session or two. Thus, the course provides a common frame of reference for faculty and majors alike and sets an intellectual agenda for the department's educational work.

I am convinced that the course is effective because its structure allows students to replicate modes of faculty learning in their own studies. The teaching fellows have the opportunity to reread a semester's worth of books and to think about how to explain them to their peers. By the end of the course, they know these works extremely well. In their small groups, students learn how to negotiate their differences to produce a collective paper. They are rarely unprepared for group meetings, because each of them will receive the grade the paper earns. Their learning takes place largely as the faculty's learning does, in conversation that results from disagreement and strives for clarity. They learn something about making an argument to people who know what they know, and about what it takes to be persuasive.

The traits of the theories course illustrate the potential of the major as a vehicle for liberal learning. Although offered only to majors and minors, the course supplies critical perspective by focusing on how the field structures arguments, how it makes its case, and how it persuades itself. By showing that core arguments of the field can be assessed (and how they can be assessed), the course demystifies such arguments and shows their constructed, tentative character. By having students learn as faculty do, teaching one another through conversation, rereading, argument, and public writing, the course illustrates how scholarship works. Exchanges among students are much more intense than those between students and faculty. Although the course employs a highly discipline-specific set of readings, it draws students into problems of inference and generalization and helps them see both the limitations and the power of specialized knowledge. Most important, the course exposes students to the field as both an intellectual and social construction. Students directly experience the complex relationship between thought and discourse, between ideas and the communities that hold them. On the basis of a course such as this, students can see the field of religion in relation to other fields. Because they have labored together to understand how their own subject works, they can begin to understand how other subjects work.

In the final analysis, the issue of the place of the major in liberal education is less a question of specialized versus general learning than of reflective and thoughtful teaching. If we draw students into the questions and problems that make a field compelling, and into the modes of argument and communication that give a field its vitality, these students can learn to be critical of their own knowledge and to understand their own role in constructing what they know. If departments become educationally thoughtful about how they engage students with their field's subjects and procedures, and if faculty become collectively responsible for the educational coherence of departmental offerings, we can have our disciplinary professionalism and liberal learning too.

References

Association of American Colleges. Integrity in the College Curriculum. Washington, D.C.: Association of American Colleges, 1985.

Boyer, E. College: The Undergraduate Experience in America. New York: HarperCollins, 1987.

Cheney, L. V. 50 Hours: A Core Curriculum for College Students. Washington, D.C.: National Endowment for the Humanities, 1989.

Kimball, B. A. "The Historical and Cultural Dimensions of the Recent Reports on Undergraduate Education." In L. F. Goodchild and H. S. Weschler (eds.), ASHE Reader on the History of Higher Education. Needham Heights, Mass.: Ginn Press, 1989.

Toulmin, S. E. Human Understanding. Vol. 1. Princeton, N.J.: Princeton University Press, 1972.

Weaver, F. S. Liberal Education. New York: Teachers College Press, 1991.

WILLIAM SCOTT GREEN is professor of religion, Philip S. Bernstein Professor of Judaic Studies, and dean of undergraduate studies, College of Arts and Science, University of Rochester.

Index

ORDERING INFORMATION

NEW DIRECTIONS FOR HIGHER EDUCATION is a series of paperback books that provides timely information and authoritative advice about major issues and administrative problems confronting every institution. Books in the series are published quarterly in Spring, Summer, Fall, and Winter and are available for purchase by subscription as well as individually.

SUBSCRIPTIONS for 1993 cost $47.00 for individuals (a savings of 25 percent over single-copy prices) and $62.00 for institutions, agencies, and libraries. Please do not send institutional checks for personal subscriptions. Standing orders are accepted.

SINGLE COPIES cost $15.95 when payment accompanies order. (California, New Jersey, New York, and Washington, D.C., residents please include appropriate sales tax.) Billed orders will be charged postage and handling.

DISCOUNTS FOR QUANTITY ORDERS are available. Please write to the address below for information.

ALL ORDERS must include either the name of an individual or an official purchase order number. Please submit your order as follows:
Subscriptions: specify series and year subscription is to begin
Single copies: include individual title code (such as HE84)

MAIL ALL ORDERS TO:
Jossey-Bass Publishers
350 Sansome Street
San Francisco, California 94104-1342

FOR SINGLE-COPY SALES OUTSIDE OF THE UNITED STATES, CONTACT:
Maxwell Macmillan International Publishing Group
866 Third Avenue
New York, New York 10022-6221

FOR SUBSCRIPTION SALES OUTSIDE OF THE UNITED STATES, contact any international subscription agency or Jossey-Bass directly.

OTHER TITLES AVAILABLE IN THE
NEW DIRECTIONS FOR HIGHER EDUCATION SERIES
Martin Kramer, Editor-in-Chief

Statement of Ownership, Management and Circulation
(Required by 39 U.S.C. 3685)

1A. Title of Publication	(ISSN)		
NEW DIRECTIONS FOR HIGHER EDUCATION	1B. PUBLICATION NO.		2. Date of Filing
	0 2 7 1 0 5 6 0		12/13/93

3. Frequency of Issue	3A. No. of Issues Published Annually	3B. Annual Subscription Price
Quarterly	Four (4)	$47.00 (personal) $62.00 (institutional)

4. Complete Mailing Address of Known Office of Publication (Street, City, County, State and ZIP+4 Code) (Not printers)

350 Sansome Street, San Francisco, CA 94104-1342 (San Francisco County)

5. Complete Mailing Address of the Headquarters of General Business Offices of the Publisher (Not printer)

(above address)

6. Full Names and Complete Mailing Address of Publisher, Editor, and Managing Editor (This item MUST NOT be blank)

Publisher (Name and Complete Mailing Address)

Jossey-Bass Inc., Publishers (above address)

Editor (Name and Complete Mailing Address)

Martin Kramer, 2807 Shasta Road, Berkeley, CA 94708

Managing Editor (Name and Complete Mailing Address)

Lynn D. Luckow, President, Jossey-Bass Inc., Publishers (address above)

7. Owner (If owned by a corporation, its name and address must be stated and also immediately thereunder the names and addresses of stockholders owning or holding 1 percent or more of total amount of stock. If not owned by a corporation, the names and addresses of the individual owners must be given. If owned by a partnership or other unincorporated firm, its name and address, as well as that of each individual must be given. If the publication is published by a nonprofit organization, its name and address must be stated.) (Item must be completed.)

Full Name	Complete Mailing Address
Macmillan, Inc.	55 Railroad Avenue Greenwich, CT 06830-6378

8. Known Bondholders, Mortgagees, and Other Security Holders Owning or Holding 1 Percent or More of Total Amount of Bonds, Mortgages or Other Securities (If there are none, so state)

Full Name	Complete Mailing Address
same as above	same as above

9. For Completion by Nonprofit Organizations Authorized To Mail at Special Rates (DMM Section 424.12 only)
The purpose, function, and nonprofit status of this organization and the exempt status for Federal income tax purposes (Check one)

(1) ☐ Has Not Changed During Preceding 12 Months (2) ☐ Has Changed During Preceding 12 Months (If changed, publisher must submit explanation of change with this statement.)

10. Extent and Nature of Circulation (See instructions on reverse side)	Average No. Copies Each Issue During Preceding 12 Months	Actual No. Copies of Single Issue Published Nearest to Filing Date
A. Total No. Copies (Net Press Run)	2,754	2,973
B. Paid and/or Requested Circulation 1. Sales through dealers and carriers, street vendors and counter sales	755	174
2. Mail Subscription (Paid and/or requested)	1,106	1,082
C. Total Paid and/or Requested Circulation (Sum of 10B1 and 10B2)	1,861	1,256
D. Free Distribution by Mail, Carrier or Other Means Samples, Complimentary, and Other Free Copies	66	66
E. Total Distribution (Sum of C and D)	1,927	1,322
F. Copies Not Distributed 1. Office use, left over, unaccounted, spoiled after printing	827	1,651
2. Return from News Agents	0	0
G. TOTAL (Sum of E, F1 and 2—should equal net press run shown in A)	2,754	2,973

11. I certify that the statements made by me above are correct and complete	Signature and Title of Editor, Publisher, Business Manager, or Owner	Larry Ishii Vice President

PS Form 3526, January 1991   (See instructions on reverse)